Ask a Little —*Learn a Lot*

How Questions Change Everything

R. W. A. Mitchell

iUniverse, Inc.
Bloomington

Ask a Little—Learn a Lot
How Questions Change Everything

iUniverse books may be ordered through booksellers or by contacting:

iUniverse
1663 Liberty Drive
Bloomington, IN 47403
www.iuniverse.com
1-800-Authors (1-800-288-4677)

ISBN: 978-1-4759-3378-9 (sc)
ISBN: 978-1-4759-3379-6 (hc)
ISBN: 978-1-4759-3380-2 (e)

Printed in the United States of America

iUniverse rev. date: 8/15/2012

About the Author

R. W. A. Mitchell was born in Toronto, Canada, and has lived there most of his life.

Mitchell holds a bachelor of science degree in physics from Queens University at Kingston and a master of science degree in nuclear physics from the University of Alberta. He pursued a career in finance and worked for several major investment banks where he created many innovative securities over two decades. He became recognized for making even the most complicated ideas easy to understand.

Mitchell knows the importance of asking questions and how much can be gleaned from asking the right ones. He will never stop being fascinated with getting inside the minds of history's greatest thinkers, question-askers, and problem solvers.

Contents

INTRODUCTION

"Learn from yesterday, live for today, hope for tomorrow.
The important thing is not to stop questioning."
— *Einstein*

HOW MUCH DO YOU think you can learn simply by asking questions?

The answer is this: more than you might ever imagine! That's because questions that no one else has asked, dreamed of asking, or perhaps even dared to ask, will lead you to *discover* things. You don't even need to dream up entirely new questions, because fresh answers to old questions have sometimes changed the world.

> "I have no special talent. I am only passionately curious."
> *Albert Einstein*

Much of what you say and think should end with question marks.

Questions are incredibly powerful tools because they lead to thinking and understanding. Questions have got us to where we are and will take us to where we're going. Most of what we take for granted in our day-to-day lives is based entirely on understanding how the world works and using it to our advantage.

> "I am curious about everything, even subjects that don't interest me."
> *Alex Trebek, Jeopardy!*

No one can really ever know where our inclination to ask questions came from, but questioning appears to be a uniquely human trait. Questions have helped us make sense of the world around us, to understand why it is the way it is, and to find an order in chaos.

We all love music, movies, and everything glamorous in popular culture. One of the goals of this book is to make ideas, thinking, and learning as glamorous as they ought to be. Albert Einstein made science and thinking cool because besides hanging out with celebrities, he became a celebrity himself, and eventually an icon of the twentieth century. Simply asking more interesting and thought-provoking questions is one of the best ways to learn more, think more, and even think more about thinking.

> "Every science begins as philosophy and ends as art."
> *Will Durant*

Thinking inspires. And with a bit of imagination, it *creates*.

Some questions, especially really good ones, might take a while to answer. Many of the questions first asked by Ancient Greek scientists and philosophers took thousands of years to answer.

Asking questions is easy. Questions can help you get inside the minds of the finest thinkers and questioners of all time, from the Ancient Greeks, to Isaac Newton and Albert Einstein. In this book, you'll see how many of the best questions ever asked spurred mankind onto its greatest achievements.

I'll always remember my first physics lecture as a college freshman. The professor opened our eyes when she asked us why we thought her course was in the Department of Arts and Science, and why wasn't there a separate Science Department. It was a while back, so I'll paraphrase her answer from memory. "While physics is a science," she said, "I want you to learn that all science is also art. The *art* lies in gaining insight into the minds of some of mankind's greatest thinkers."

> "The beautiful thing about learning is that no one can take it away from you."
> *B. B. King*

That's what this book is about.

It's meant to be lively, fun, and easy to read. It includes examples of some of the best questions ever asked, illustrated with examples from a wide range of topics, including everything from mathematics and science, to philosophy, game theory, gambling, lucky numbers, and even game shows.

Inside, you'll explore questions based on the following:

- learning how to learn, just by asking questions
- the kinds of questions asked by the greatest thinkers
- paradoxes, which are rather peculiar and tricky questions
- how to surf the North Pole
- how to type like a monkey
- how to win on *Let's Make a Deal*
- the weird science of Wile E. Coyote
- messing around in boats
- how to sell valuable baseball cards
- how to get ketchup out of the darned bottle
- the biggest number (or is it numbers?)
- supersonic dinosaurs (what?)
- why a chicken might cross the road
- dropping watermelons from very high places
- snail racing (they turn out to be relatively fast)
- unexpected results from flipping coins
- how to get lucky

We're thinking all the time—even when we're asleep. If you can turn just a bit more of your thinking into good questions, you will be amazed by the results.

> "Who questions much, shall learn much, and retain much."
> *Francis Bacon*

You don't need any special skills other than an open mind and a willingness to always ask. There aren't any formulas, and there isn't any tricky math in here, because in the words of Stephen Hawking, "Someone once told me that each equation I included in the book would halve the sales."

Start right now by getting into the habit of always asking questions.

Become skeptical. Question anything and everything in the world around you, and the world within you. There's never any shortage of good questions to ask, and no shortage of bad ones either. But as a friend of mine once said, "The only stupid question is the one you don't ask."

So read on and ask away.

At the end of each chapter, you'll find keywords to search in case you want to dig a little deeper. Some are factual and some are silly, because life should be fun. You can also find lots of useful YouTube videos by searching the same keywords.

Web Search Keywords

| *fun science* | *asking questions* | *stephen hawking* | *she blinded me with science thomas dolby* | *steven wright quotes* |

Chapter 1

Ask Away!

"To raise new questions, new possibilities, to regard old problems from a new angle, requires creative imagination and marks real advance in science."
—*Einstein*

THE BEST WAY TO explore new ideas comes by simply asking questions. When you ask questions, you learn things. It naturally follows that the more questions you ask, the more you can learn. Many of your thoughts and much of what you say should end with question marks.

"Ask not what your country can do for you—ask what you can do for your country."
JFK

Question anything and everything about the world around you. When you learn to ask questions that no one else ever asked, thought of asking, or perhaps dared to ask, I guarantee you will start on a path that will lead you to amazing discoveries for yourself, and quite possibly for the rest of us too.

In life, you will always be presented with ideas put to you as facts. Why believe any of it without asking and thinking? The danger of not questioning and not thinking for oneself comes from one of the most disturbing, yet compelling, quotes from one scary man:

"What luck for rulers, that men do not think."
—*Hitler*

Around the beginning of the twentieth century, there were amazing changes going on in the sciences, physics in particular. Old ideas were challenged, and many of the new ones turned hundreds, and even thousands, of years of thinking on its head. You'll read about the revolutionary ideas of modern physics in later chapters.

One important question came up in the art world in the early 1900s after the invention of the camera. Prior to photography, the *best* artists were those who could draw or paint the most lifelike representations of interesting subjects. After the camera arrived and its technology had been refined, artists and critics started to ask themselves, "What is the point of art if we can just take a picture instead?" This simple question gave rise to new meaning in the world of art and ushered in the age of modern art. Art was not just about representing images anymore. Art became about *new* ways of looking at subjects.

Photography eventually became an art form in itself. In fine art photography, images come from the creative vision of the photographers. They often make use of unique perspectives and fresh ways of capturing even the most commonplace subjects. Photographs taken by American photographer Ansel Adams, which are black-and-white images of the American West, especially in Yosemite National Park, are truly remarkable and focused on the way he perceived light.

"If at first, the idea is not absurd, then there is no hope for it."
Albert Einstein

This new way of thinking, by reexamining old ideas and questioning them, spilled over into other disciplines and spawned even more revolutions in the arts.

In classical music, most composers at the turn of the twentieth century continued on in the tradition of nineteenth-century music. As modernism grew increasingly important, composers such as Mahler, Debussy, and Stravinsky began to produce music with new forms, timbres, and orchestration. Electronic music made its debut later, when composers began to move away from the classical sounds of stringed instruments. It started with the Theremin. This odd instrument was used in the *Star Trek* theme song and continues to be featured in many other contemporary tracks.

Modern jazz would come later, based on new ways of looking at and reinterpreting traditional jazz. Miles Davis became one of the greatest questioners of the interpretation of jazz. He completely changed what the music was all about, not once, but *four* times.

> "All great truths begin as blasphemies."
> *George Bernard Shaw*

Much of the rock music in the late 1960s and early 1970s, by performers such as Jimi Hendrix and Led Zeppelin, were about reinterpreting the blues.

Modern architecture completely reinterpreted classic design. Years later it gave rise to striking new structures from designers like Frank Lloyd Wright, followed by others like Frank Gehry. If you've never seen it, look up images of Bilbao, the Guggenheim museum in Spain. If that wasn't a new way of looking at architecture, I don't know what is.

In modern dance, choreographers began to move away from classical ballet to a more creative self-expression, just as happened in other arts.

Some really *big* questions had come up many years before. There were amazing discoveries in the 1800s, and many more were to follow. James Clerk Maxwell explained how electricity and magnetism work in the late 1800s. Electrical currents in wires make them act like magnets, and moving magnets inside coils of wire induces currents. His big question must have been something like, "Why do electricity and magnetism seem to be connected?" By answering it, he went on to develop the theory of electromagnetism, perhaps the greatest breakthrough of nineteenth-century science.

There were other great discoveries in the making back then. Robert Chambers, who was a journalist—and no doubt a great question asker—published *Vestiges of the Natural History of Creation*. In it, he asked where all the different species came from, and proposed that some transmutation between species must be happening. His theories were very unpopular with both the church and scientists at the time. A few years later, Charles Darwin published *On the Origin of the Species* and explained evolution. He felt that Chambers's work prepared the public mind for Darwin's own later theories of natural selection. Chambers asked; Darwin answered.

To learn by asking questions, you have to ask the right ones.

> "I only ask good questions."
> *Judge Judy*

The first step is to understand what makes up a good question. The word *why* is one of the most important and powerful words in the English language—except for *me*. Just kidding, of course.

I had the good fortune to have a high school English teacher who was brilliant, yet subtle. One of the best lessons I took away from his teaching was something he called the *Five Qs*, which are key words that trigger important questions to ask. They are the following:

- Who
- What
- Where
- When
- Why

To that he added: "and sometimes *How*." Maybe it should have been: "and sometimes *Why*." He was an English teacher, after all.

These simple questions are very powerful tools.

Their strength lies in focusing your thinking. Sometimes it's a good idea just to jot them down on a blank sheet of paper when you're thinking, learning, writing, or trying to solve a problem. You may have noticed that the Five Qs are all *open-ended* questions that lead to further consideration or discussion. This is in stark contrast to *closed-ended* questions that can be answered simply with a yes or no. Closed-ended questions don't usually lead to any dialogue. Conversations don't start with a question like, "Do you like books?" "What kind of books do you like?" fares far better. Some even say that any question that begins with a word like *did* is a dud. Nevertheless, closed-ended questions can serve a purpose. Besides, you can always follow up a dud with a *why*.

My teacher's ideas struck me as conveying a very common-sense approach to gathering information and knowledge. While he was a gifted man and great teacher, it turns out that his method was by no means new or original. Thankfully, he jazzed it up a bit to make it fun and interesting for us. Its origins date all the way back to classical Greek philosophy, when Socrates (around 400 BC) inspired the Socratic method, which is teaching based on asking and answering questions. The idea is to generate a dialogue that stimulates thinking that guides students to answers.

> "The most valuable commodity I know of is information."
> *Wall Street*

These kinds of questions form the basis of legal education and newspaper reporting. Reporters always ask these questions to get to the bottom of a story, and the answers form the basis of their articles. The next time you pick up a newspaper, see if you can spot it in practice. The same approach is also widely used in police and detective work.

If you're familiar with the game *Clue*, a popular board game that was invented in 1944, you'll recognize three Qs necessary to solve the puzzle: *who*, *where*, and *how*. The game is based on a murder mystery where someone is murdered in a mansion. There are six suspects and six potential murder weapons. The game progresses as players move from room to room trying to gather clues. In the end, when players who think they've solved the mystery ask three questions like: "Was it Miss Scarlet, in the kitchen, with a knife?"

The idea of the five (or six) Qs first gained popular attention with a poem written by Rudyard Kipling in 1902. He went on to win the Nobel Prize in Literature in 1907. Among his many other stories, he is best known for *Jungle Book*, which was eventually adapted into a popular Disney film.

The five Ws (and one H) appear in his *Just So Stories* as follows:

I Keep six honest serving-men
(They taught me all I knew);
Their names are What and Why and When
And How and Where and Who.
I send them over land and sea,
I send them east and west;
But after they have worked for me,
I give them all a rest.
I let them rest from nine till five,
For I am busy then,
As well as breakfast, lunch, and tea,
For they are hungry men.
But different folk have different views;
I know a person small—
She keeps ten million serving-men,
Who get no rest at all!
She sends 'em abroad on her own affairs,
From the second she opens her eyes—
One million Hows, two million Wheres,
And seven million Whys!
—*The Elephant's Child*

Toyota Motor Corporation has five Ws. They contributed significantly to the company's manufacturing success through a chain of continuous improvement. In this case, the Ws are all *whys*. By stringing them together in a coherent sequence, they helped lead the company to the root of problems. For example, "Why is it broken?" leads to "Why did it break in the first place?" and so on. *Why* is still viewed by Toyota as a fundamental business tool. The same approach has since been adopted by many other companies and people.

Brilliant and inspired minds have asked lots of questions over the years. Many questions first asked long ago have determined how we got to where we are today. Some date as far back as the Ancient Greeks. Nevertheless, good questions always deserve to be re-asked and re-answered, because sometimes, fresh answers to old questions can lead to great discoveries.

If you take the time to ask good questions and come up with excellent answers, you will shine.

Web Search Keywords
| *asking questions* | *five basic types of questions* | *asking all them questions* | *who's on first* | *sesame street asking questions* |

Chapter 2

Questions: Not a Trivial Pursuit

People love questions—it's in our nature. Mankind has an insatiable thirst for knowledge.

Questioning appears to be a uniquely human trait. Primates, such as gorillas and chimpanzees, have been taught to communicate using sign language or by picking out tokens that represent words. Sarah, Washoe, and Koko are among the best-known examples. They learned to answer questions such as *who*, *what*, and *where*; but they never actually *asked* any despite understanding the signs or tokens that stood for questions. This is in stark contrast to children who ask questions ceaselessly. They start asking one-word questions even at the earliest stages of speech, just by using intonation: "Out?" They've also been known to say: "Out! Out! Out!"

People like to be asked questions and to come up with answers. It happens all around us and leads to a sense of accomplishment in our work, at least on a good day. We even like answering questions for entertainment. Asking questions is not trivial by any means; it's a vital part of our lives.

Questions form the basis of much of our popular culture. Observational comedy often starts with a question like: "Have you ever noticed how…?" In the pilot episode of *Seinfeld* (you can find the script on the show's official website), I count at least one question in sixty-six of the two hundred lines spoken by the cast. That's about 30 percent. Talk show hosts and talk radio people always ask loads of questions.

If you attune yourself to listening for questions, it's amazing how many there are swirling around all the time. Most are so mundane that we pay no attention.

- What time is it?
- What are your specials?
- What other colors does this come in?
- You want how much?!

In a way, competitive sports events answer questions. The Olympic motto is "Faster, higher, stronger." The games resolve to answer the questions "Who is the fastest … ?'"

McDonalds currently serves more than sixty million customers every day, and they've made billions of dollars by asking one simple question: "Do you want fries with that?"

If McDonalds asks that of every customer, it would amount to about twenty-two billion questions a year. That's not only a lot of questions, it's a great way to sell fries. Why stop at fries? "Would you like to supersize that?" was hugely successful, and inspired the fast food documentary *Supersize Me*.

The enormously popular *Guinness World Records* (previously *The Guinness Book of World Records)* is a reference book that contains a collection of world records on just about any topic you might imagine. *Guinness World Records* is now recognized as *the* authority on verifying and keeping track of world records. The book itself is recognized as being the best-selling copyrighted book of all time, with sales exceeding one hundred million copies. It's also reputed to be one of the most frequently stolen books from US public libraries. Believe it or not, the Bible

> "I went into a McDonalds yesterday and said, 'I'd like some fries.' The girl at the counter said, 'Would you like fries with that?'"
> *Jay Leno*

makes that list as well. I guess the thieves should read up on "Thou shall not steal."

As the story goes, the idea for the Guinness book came from Sir Hugh Beaver on a hunting trip in Ireland in 1951. A debate raged at dinner over whether or not the fastest game bird in Europe was the golden plover. It came up because the hunters in the party who had failed to shoot one tried using its speed as an excuse. They soon concluded that it was impossible to find the answer. It occurred to Sir Hugh that these kinds of debates were probably going on all the time, particularly in pubs in the UK. He was Managing Director of Guinness Breweries at the time, which owned thousands of pubs. After years of collecting information, the first edition was published in 1955 and quickly became a bestseller. Oddly, the answer to the question that sparked the book didn't appear on its pages until the thirty-sixth edition (1989). The fastest game bird turned out to be the red grouse, which was measured to be slightly faster than the plover.

Entire entertainment industries were inspired by the success of the Guinness book. Trivia books started to appear in the 1960s and continue to grow in popularity. I recently looked up an online bookseller and counted more than two hundred different trivia books for sale. There are also many trivia games available as computer games, on the Internet and in games like *Buzztime,* which is popular in pubs and bars across North America.

"Why is it trivia? People call it trivia because they know nothing and are embarrassed about it."
Robbie Coltrane

Game shows involve answering questions or solving puzzles. They have held a place in American popular culture beginning with radio shows such as *Spelling Bee* and *Truth or Consequences* in the late 1930s and 1940s. Some of the shows were made into television programs, and more were created as the medium of TV caught on.

Twenty One was a popular quiz show in the late 1950s that featured two competitors, a challenger and a champion, who answered multiple-choice questions in separate booths with headphones on.

It ended badly when it was discovered that the show was rigged. Well-liked champions were being passed the correct answers during the program to ensure they won in order to return the following week and help boost ratings. The film *Quiz Show* is based on the scandal.

The $64,000 Question was another popular 1950s quiz show. Its name was based on *The $64 Question,* which was a radio show in the 1940s. The expression, "That's the sixty-four dollar question" came into widespread use at the time to describe challenging questions and problems.

In the end, quiz shows of that era fell out of favor in the aftermath of the *Twenty One* scandal. Nevertheless, quiz shows managed to stage a comeback. *Jeopardy!* has been popular since its debut in 1964 and features trivia questions about history, literature, the arts, geography, popular culture, science, and sports. The show has a unique answer-and-question format, where contestants are given answers as clues and have to come up with the corresponding questions.

It seems that asking and answering questions really can be fun for us.

How else could you explain the popularity of board games like Trivial Pursuit? It's one of the best-selling board games of all time. *Time* magazine called it the biggest phenomenon in game history. The game is based on answering trivia questions from a range of six categories. It's so popular that the game has become entrenched in our culture, much like Monopoly. It even appears in *Seinfeld* (in the episode "The Bubble Boy") where George's game with the bubble boy ends in a struggle. George disputes his answer to the question, "Who invaded Spain in the eighth century?" The bubble boy correctly answers, "The Moors," but the question card reads "Moops" due to a misprint. When George refuses to accept the answer, the bubble boy attacks him. These sorts of misprints and factual errors have come up in a number of lawsuits over the years where

> "I think it's wrong that only one company makes the game Monopoly."
> *Steven Wright*

writers of trivia books have claimed that misspellings and other errors were deliberately included in their books to spot copyright infringements. None of the claims against Trivial Pursuit have stood up in court.

Have you ever noticed how much kids enjoy silly questions and riddles?

You can always tell if a riddle will be a hit with the under-eight set if it makes you groan. Here are a few examples:

- Why did the boy throw the clock out of the window? (*To see time fly*)
- What kind of tie does a ghost wear at a party? (*A boo-tie*)
- What kind of stones does Frankenstein have in his collection? (*Tombstones*)

The examples can go on and on, and are beneficial to learning because kids have fun juggling between the sense and nonsense. They also exercise imaginations and promote creative thinking.

Closely related to riddles are trick questions. They are intended to make you believe you should answer them in one way, when the real question is buried somewhere inside. There aren't any precise formal definitions that let you distinguish between the two. If you look at a book (or website) of riddles and compare them to trick questions, you will find a fair amount of overlap. The biggest thing they have in common is that both certainly take some ingenuity to answer. Riddles are best described as involving some kind of pun or incongruity ("to see time fly") while trick questions often have easy, seemingly obvious answers but are usually written in such a way as to trick the reader. Examples of hidden meanings behind trick questions include:

> Reporter: "How did you find America?"
> John: "Turn left at Greenland."
> *The Beatles*

- Why are 2011 pennies worth more than 2010 pennies? (*2011 is one more penny than 2010 pennies.*)
- What happened in 1961 and will not happen again until 6009? (*Both still read as numbers if you turn them upside down, and 6009 is the next one after 1961.*)
- Is it legal for a man to marry his widow's sister? (*Dead men can't get married.*)
- When is four one-half of five? (*If you take the IV in five as Roman numerals, it makes up half the word F(IV)E.*)

And then there is every young child's favorite: silly questions. They exhibit a complete lack of common sense, which makes them foolish and fun. In the *Cat's Quizzer*, the Cat in the Hat challenges very young readers with seemingly silly questions such as: "Do pineapples grow on pine trees or apple trees?"

> "I bought some powdered water but didn't know what to add to it."
> *Steven Wright*

Small and seemingly trivial questions can sometimes lead to much bigger and important ones. In the end, the real trick is to make even the most challenging questions about difficult topics both interesting and fun.

Web Search Keywords

| *koko gorilla* | *sarah chimp* | *supersize* | *guinness book* | *64000 question* | *trivial pursuit* | *jeopardy* | *seinfeld bubble boy* | *seussville* | *geico rhetorical questions commercial* | *what's my line youtube* |

Chapter 3

A Good Question about Questions

One good question to ask about questions is "How many different ways are there to ask them?"

The simplest questions are intended to gather information as in, "What is the capital of Canada?" In addition to the Five Qs, many questions start with words like *which*, *does*, and *is*. They not only represent the most basic form of learning but led to the scientific method, where questioning fits in between observing something and explaining how it could be so with a theory.

Questioning is fundamental to the justice system. Leading and loaded questions sometimes come up in trials. They can lead or trick a defendant into a desired answer by including some assumption of guilt. Leading questions try to direct an answer: "You were near the crime scene, weren't you?" The non-leading version would be, "Where were you on the night of the crime?" The most common example of a loaded question is this: "Have you stopped beating your wife?" There is no correct response, because both yes and no answers result in some admission of guilt. The only way to answer a question like that is to turn it around or rephrase it. "I have never beaten my wife," would be a good reply. Courtroom judges, we hope, are always on the lookout for these kinds of questions.

Surveys and polls are all about questioning. They are used to gain an understanding of people's views and preferences by sampling a small group of people and applying what they learn to a larger population. Public opinion surveys and polls frequently cover topics such as:

- Politics (predicting the likely outcome of an election)
- Behavior (measuring lifestyle choices such as smoking)
- Economics (income and spending)
- Science (particularly regarding health-care issues)
- Marketing (how best to sell products)

Surveys pose questions requiring a yes or no response, selecting from a list (multiple-choice), scales (strongly agree … don't care … strongly disagree), or ranking agreement on a numeric scale such as from one to ten.

The most broadly-based survey is the census. Governments perform them to collect information about their populations. They usually take place on a regular schedule to provide an official count of population and its demographics. The census dates back many thousands of years, all the way to ancient China and appears several times in the Bible. The Roman Empire made extensive use of them as well, and the word itself is derived from Latin.

Focus groups are used extensively in marketing, where participants are usually paid for their opinions. In them, individuals in the group express their perceptions and opinions about products, services, concepts, advertisements, ideas, and packaging. Focus groups are intended to turn into group discussions about a given question, making them less rigid than a survey. The value added by focus groups has been a matter of some debate because they have occasionally led to the introduction of products, such as New Coke, that subsequently became major failures.

When is a question not really a question?

First, there are imperative sentences, which are written like questions, but are not really intended to be questions at all. They are simply requests for some action such as, "Could I trouble you for the salt?"

There are also rhetorical questions that are meant to make a point by asking. Rhetorical questions don't expect or even want an answer. They are most often used in speeches and lead listeners to arrive at the speaker's point of view for themselves. In Monty Python's *Life of Brian,* there is a line that asks, "What have the Romans ever done for us?" It makes listeners think, "The Romans have never done anything for us." That comes across more persuasively than simply stating the point.

> "All right, the aqueduct, the sanitation, and the roads. I'll give them that."
> *Monty Python*

Rhetoric can also be used sarcastically with simple questions like: "Can't you do anything right?" or "Shouldn't you be working?" One commonly used sarcastic question is "Who knew?" which implies that the preceding statement should have been utterly obvious. "Smoking can lead to lung cancer. Who knew?" Rhetorical questions have also been used to set out on some course of action. "Hey, why not?" has probably led to more than its fair share of misadventures.

Sometimes it takes a rhetorical question to answer a rhetorical question. In the musical *The Sound of Music*, the question in the song *Maria*, "How do you solve a problem like Maria?" is answered with other questions like: "How do you catch a cloud and pin it down?" and "How do you hold a moonbeam in your hand?"

One of the most familiar forms of questioning, sometimes dreaded by students, has got to be multiple-choice.

This form of testing was first used to assess the intelligence of World War I military recruits. Sarcastic students often refer to them as multiple-guess tests. The easiest way to fix the flaw that rewards guessing is by scoring a blank response with zero, and introducing a penalty for an incorrect answer. SATs, for example, subtract one-quarter point for incorrect answers.

The $64,000 question about multiple-choice questions has to be about changing answers. "Should I stay with my initial answer or switch if I reconsider?" Conventional wisdom suggests you should always stick with your first choice. After numerous studies, it turns out that you are far better off to switch, but only after *careful* reconsideration. Some believe that the popular misconception of never switching arises from the *von Restorff effect*. It accounts for how our memories are stronger for standout events. The idea is that if you go back and check your scoring, incorrect answers that came after making a switch are more memorable than those where the correct switch was made.

> "Our sins are more easily remembered than our good deeds."
> *Democritus*

You can find all kinds of questions anywhere you look.

Web Search Keywords

| *monty python romans* | *how do you solve a problem like maria* | *bill cosby new coke* | *von restorff effect* |

Chapter 4

A Good Question about Thinking

How many thoughts do you think you have in a day?

That's a pretty tough one because it begs the question: "What exactly is a thought?"

When you think about all the information we're constantly being bombarded with, just from our senses alone, there has to be an absolutely mind-boggling amount of thinking going on inside our heads every second of every minute of every day.

However, there's thinking and then there's *thinking,* and our minds are capable of thinking in all kinds of different ways. This book is about ideas, concepts, and the kind of complicated mental activity that leads to questions. Those are the kinds of thoughts we'd like to understand, so to cut down on any confusion, let's call them *complex thoughts.*

We are not machines, and our minds don't work like computers, but perhaps an analogy based on them isn't such a bad idea. Computers are made up of hardware and software. The human version of hardware is our brains' ability to process information. The speed limit for this kind of thinking is like the processor speed of a computer chip. Complex thoughts come from

> "Oh the thinks you can think if only you try."
> *Dr. Seuss*

the software part and are fantastically complicated. Even though our hardware is incredibly fast, the kinds of complex thoughts it takes to ask questions must require an extraordinary number of steps in our mental programming code. Using the computer analogy again, even though a chess-playing supercomputer is processing information at an astonishing rate, it can take quite a while to come up with its next move.

The simplest form of thinking is responding to a stimulus. An *orienting response* is an instinctive reaction to something. The term was coined by Ivan Pavlov (of "Pavlov's dog" fame) and describes an involuntary response that is hardwired into us. Say there's a loud noise somewhere nearby. Without thinking, we are compelled to turn toward it to see what it was. We respond first and save the *real* thinking for later. We're all born with it—clap your hands and a baby will look. Orienting responses are everywhere in nature. Sharks have a sense that detects vibrations in the water and makes them instinctively turn toward a thrashing fish (or the swimmers in the film *Jaws*). In a noisy and flashy world, this response would drive us crazy if we didn't learn to tune out familiar noises, as explained by Eugene Soklov's *habituation* or *familiarity effect*.

There is a branch of experimental psychology known as *mental chronometry* (from the Greek *chronos*, meaning "time"). It studies the reaction time between seeing or hearing something and responding to it, although it could apply equally well to our other senses too. The simplest kind of experiment to gauge reaction time would be something like measuring how long it takes you to press a button after a light goes on. That can give us an idea of the processing speed of the brain. Reactions that require more thinking can be measured by including a number of differently colored lights and pressing the button only when a certain color (or combination of colors) flashes. There's no end to the kinds of tasks where response times can easily be measured. The goals of these types of experiments include understanding how the mind processes information and how different tasks have differing response times, depending on how much thinking is involved. By using the reaction time of the simplest task as a benchmark, the timing of more complicated tasks gives insight into how fast our minds are capable of thinking in more and more complicated situations.

Processing and performing simple tasks are one thing, but the kind of complex thinking that leads to ideas and questioning is quite another. Read a book. Look at art. Listen to music. Look at art while listening to music. Look at a sunset while driving a car with the stereo on. You get the idea.

All five of our senses can trigger floods of powerful memories, thoughts, and ideas. None of this even includes any of the complicated thinking we do in our minds just sitting alone and daydreaming in a dimly lit room. If you ever have trouble sleeping, doesn't it sometimes feel like your mind is racing? *Racing mind* is a condition that can be triggered by anything from stress to sleep deprivation or certain other disorders. If you ever experience it, you'll see just how fast your mind is capable of jumping around between random thoughts, images, music, and recollections of things people have said to you.

"Madness is to think of too many things in succession too fast, or of one thing too excessively."
Voltaire

One kind of thinking we're always doing is recognizing patterns in all the information that comes from our senses. We process visual sensations like objects, faces and pictures, as well as sounds, smells, and tastes at an astonishing speed. Consider the simple act of looking at a photograph of a tree. To your eyes, it's just a smear of patterns and colors, but you instantly recognize it as a tree. A monkey jumping around in a room still looks like a monkey to you, even when it starts hanging upside down from a chandelier. Sounds work the same way. In action movies, I can recognize the distinct bursts of machine-gun fire at twenty rounds per second. Similarly, we can recognize distinct images up to twelve or fifteen frames per second. Movies are shot at around thirty frames per second, and the separate images blend together and appear as motion. How long does it take you to smell or taste something?

"Oh God; it's so hot. And what is that smell?"
Seinfeld

When something isn't immediately recognizable, it takes more thinking. People's minds seem to be naturally programmed to try to make sense out of all the chaos that our senses perceive. If you've never visited a disorganized junk shop, try it and you'll see what I mean. Take a look around and you will be flooded with so much visual stimulation that it's almost overwhelming. Not only are you looking at all that junk, your mind is going into overdrive trying to figure out what everything is and what you might want to do with it. In the 1990s, computer-generated 3D posters became popular. If you stared into the patterns long enough, objects eventually materialized in front of your eyes.

Why do you think *Where's Waldo?* became so popular? If you were to describe it simply for what it is—picking out a peculiar looking character from a sea of similar characters—you might wonder why anybody would ever be interested. However, when you actually look at a Waldo puzzle, they're fascinating. Kids of all ages love Waldo because it challenges their minds to sort through all the clutter. What started as a children's book now even comes as a smart phone application for all the big kids out there.

> "Out of clutter find simplicity."
> *Albert Einstein*

The game *Scrabble*, which has been popular since 1948, is even bigger. It involves finding order out of seven scrambled letter tiles. You have to combine them into words and also make the most out of them by deciding where best to place them on the board. Word jumbles, word search puzzles, and jigsaw puzzles are popular for the same reasons.

There is a great trick that you might be able to use when it comes to unscrambling groups of letters. It might even give some insight into how minds work. If you were given a sequence of letters such as:

| O | T | C | R | U | Y | N |,

Seeing word combinations might be pretty hard to do right away, because it immediately calls on the left side of our brains that is usually associated with linear thinking.

Instead, try to scramble the letters in space. That gets the creative right brain engaged. Try it like this:

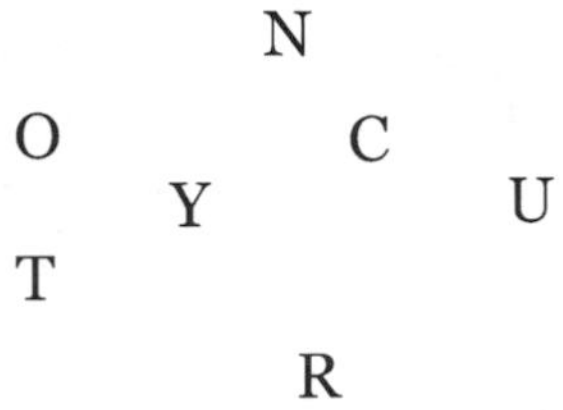

Try the first way for a minute. If you give up on it, try to come up with words when the letters are messed up. It illustrates the difference between left- and right-brain thinking, and might be something that helps you some day.

It turns out that there are sixty-nine possible words from that combination of letters with only one seven-letter solution. Several of the longer words are listed at the end of the chapter.

Our apparent need to organize information may also partly account for why many people become passionate about abstract art. Some modern art can take a while to understand what the artist's image is referring to. One good example is the work of abstract expressionist Jackson Pollock. He eventually became known as "Jack the Dripper" because he painted by dripping paint onto a canvas lying on the floor. These kinds of works can be quite mesmerizing. Pollock's eight-foot-by-four-foot painting named *No. 5* (1948) sold for $140 million to record mogul David Geffen in 2006. Although Pollock's works might look chaotic, it turns out that there actually is order and structure in them—the same kind we see in nature all around us. *Chaos theory* comes up in chapter 30.

Recognizing that our brains are always thinking extraordinarily quickly, we need to make some assumptions to get at least some idea of how many complex thoughts we're capable of having in a day. Let's say we do our complex thinking at a rate *at least* as fast as what we typically communicate at by reading, writing, speaking, or listening.

None of what follows pretends to be any kind of scientific or academic argument, and while it's far less than perfect, at least it's somewhere to start. Call communication a benchmark for complex thought. And if you disagree, a good question to think about it is this: "If we can think about what to say or understand much faster than we actually communicate, why don't we all talk faster?"

Speech and reading are intertwined. As children, we learn to speak before we learn to read. The first step to reading is to read out loud. Later, we learn to *subvocalize* by speaking silently to ourselves. When we read, write, think of something to say, or reason something out we usually speak silently to ourselves. Subvocalization is an integral part of complex thinking tasks such as comprehension and memorization. It actually triggers nerves to fire and stimulates the muscles associated with speech, as if we were talking out loud. We never even notice it, although some people do move their lips very slightly. NASA scientists have been working on interpreting these signals through electrodes (detectors) attached to skin near the throat. These electrodes make use of software to recognize the patterns that correspond to speech and convert them into text, much like voice-recognition software.

To use communication as an analogy of complex thought, our first step is to establish how fast we communicate.

Average adults read at a rate of 200 to 250 words per minute (WPM), though some speed-readers claim to read at rates that exceed thousands of WPM.

Speed-readers usually train themselves not to subvocalize, but their speed comes at the cost of greatly reduced comprehension and retention. That makes their *effective* reading rate much slower.

Steve Woodmore of the UK is regarded as the world's fastest talker at 637 WPM, but we generally like to listen at a rate of only about 150 WPM. Not surprisingly, that's the rate that audio books are typically played at. The speech function in my computer read out

> "The trouble with talking too fast is that you may say something you haven't thought of yet."
> *Ann Landers*

this page at a rate of 151 WPM. Auctioneers sound like they're speaking incredibly quickly. That's because they use *filler*—nonsense and repeated words between the important pieces of information. When you strip away all the filler, they're actually passing on prices at a rate of only about 40 WPM. That makes sense, because bidders need time to think about the prices and how much they're willing to pay, which likely involves more thought than just listening to a story.

We write at only about 25 WPM, though speed writers, who use phonetic abbreviations like *kwk* for *quick*, can reach speeds of 80 to 120 WPM. Shorthand, which seems to be a long-forgotten art, can get up to rates of about 200 WPM. Proficient typists are able to type at 50 WPM, while Barbara Blackburn holds the record for typing (on a real typewriter) at 150 WPM for minutes, with shorter sprints up to 212 WPM. Speed records with computer keyboards are faster still, with 242 WPM set by Guilherme Sandrini of Brazil. His record is actually closer to 290 WPM on most scales, though, because it was based on a definition of six characters per word, compared to the customary five. The American Sign Language alphabet (A–Z) has been signed in 5.13 seconds, which corresponds to about 60 WPM.

To illustrate communication in musical terms, we seem to like to listen at about the same rates as speech. If you measure the speed of music in beats per minute (BPM), you'll find that most classical music ranges from *adagio* (slowly and stately, at seventy BPM) to *presto* (very fast, at up 200 BPM). In contemporary music, house music runs generally at around 125 BPM, while dance runs to about 150 BPM. Jazz from the fast bebop era of the 1940s and 1950s, which featured the likes of Charlie Parker, sometimes played at around 380 BPM. That can make it challenging for some listeners.

Getting back to the original question of how many thoughts we have in a day, let's say that we subvocalize much of our complex thinking into sentences of information.

Even if we digest information at a rate of only 200 WPM, that would amount to 12,000 words per hour. If an average sentence consists of fifteen words, which is recommended by many book publishers, it corresponds to a rate of 800 sentences per hour. Assume much of that is wasted. Thoughts like "It's hot in here" don't count for our purposes, except for the one time that led to the invention of the air-conditioner. Say only 25 percent of those thought sentences amount to meaningful thoughts or ideas. That would amount to 200 complex thoughts per hour, or 3,200 complex thoughts per day (in our sixteen waking hours). Of course, this doesn't include any thinking you do when you're asleep, which many psychiatrists would argue is quite a lot.

The important point of all this is that if we could convert even just 5 percent more of all those thoughts into questions, it would amount to 160 questions per day, or just under 60,000 questions in a year. Let's say it takes that one-in-a-million question to lead to some breakthrough or significant new idea. That would take, on average, about seventeen years to ask. And while that might sound like a long time, it really isn't when you consider that two of Einstein's greatest theories (special and general relativity) each took him about seven years of thinking to complete.

Asking questions has always paid off, and the ones that take a while to come up with are often the best ones to ask.

Web Search Keywords
| *pavlov's dog* | *jaws trailer* | *where's waldo* | *scrabble* | *jackson pollock no. 5* | *fastest talker* | *fastest auctioneer* |

Seven-letter solution: country
Others include: county, outcry, cornu, corny, count, court, crony, cyton, runty, uncoy…

Chapter 5

Questions That Moved the World

Around the year 1500, some seemingly new ideas started popping up. Many of them were not really new at all, but had been rediscovered by re-asking and re-answering the same questions from a long time before.

People believed back then that the earth was the center of everything, and the sun, planets, and stars all revolved around us, because we were *so* important. Go figure.

They should have asked, "Why should everything revolve around us, and how can we even know if it's true?"

Copernicus proposed that, based on his observations, it all might work the other way around, that the earth and planets revolve around the sun. It was a shocking idea at the time. But it was by no means new, having already been proposed by Greek astronomer Aristarchus, who lived around 200 BC.

> "And let's face it. Without rules, there's chaos."
> *Seinfeld*

Later, Galileo invented the telescope and began to measure all things astronomical. Armed with his accurate measurements of the motions of the earth, the moon, and the planets, everything started to make sense. There *was* an order to the motion of the heavens, and Copernicus had been right after all. The only object that revolved around the earth was the moon. The earth and rest of the planets all revolved around the sun. It turned out to be a good-news, bad-news story for Galileo though. The good news was that it was a splendid idea and was, in fact, correct. The bad news was it didn't exactly match up with the popular religious views of the time, and he was convicted on charges of heresy for teaching it. In 2000, the Vatican issued a formal apology for the mix-up and built a statue in his honor, which stands within the Vatican walls. Eventually, all these advances in astronomy had a huge impact in navigation that triggered great voyages to explore the globe.

While there were enormous advances made over the ensuing years, let's fast-forward to the 1950s, not really all that long ago, when an astronomer named Edwin Hubble made some truly remarkable discoveries. He showed us that we live in a universe that has more galaxies than there are stars in our own galaxy. Perhaps more startling was that the galaxies are all moving apart from each other at alarming speeds.

> "The universe is expanding. That should ease the traffic."
> *Steven Wright*

Look at the sky from your bedroom window, and you see mostly stars in our galaxy, the Milky Way. It looks like a band of light across the sky unless you live in a brightly lit city, in which case it's pretty hard to spot. If you live in the country, however, and happen to spot a far-away galaxy, it's moving away from you. We realized a long time ago that we're not the center of the solar system or the galaxy, let alone the universe. So how can everything possibly be moving away from everything else at the same time?

One way people have tried to picture this is by imagining that all the galaxies are like dots sitting on the surface of a giant balloon, and God is blowing it up. As it inflates, the dots all move apart from each other. Hubble not only discovered that all the galaxies are moving away from each other, but the farther they are apart, the faster they're moving away.

> "Science without religion is lame, religion without science is blind."
> *Albert Einstein*

The Hubble space telescope was put into orbit in 1990, and has taken absolutely amazing photographs of stars, galaxies, and objects that are unimaginable distances away. Its crystal clear images are possible because the earth's atmosphere doesn't get in the way, which would otherwise blur everything. Our atmosphere is the reason why stars twinkle.

One interesting fact about the Hubble is that after years of design, construction, and finally the launch, the images came out blurred. It must have been a huge letdown to everyone at NASA when the first images began to arrive. I bet the scientists and the manufacturer asked what possibly could have gone wrong. Eventually, it was decided that there must have been some defect in the main mirror. After a lot of thought, someone came up with a great idea. Perhaps a giant contact lens could be constructed for the optics. Three years later, the space shuttle *Endeavour* was launched, and the astronauts installed the lens. The prescription worked perfectly, and the patient was cured.

You can see some awesome pictures at hubblesite.org.

Since then, many astronomers started asking, "With all the recent advancements in technology, can't there now be a way to do all this from the ground?" Indeed there is.

A European group intends to build their E-ELT, which stands for European Extremely Large Telescope, on top of a mountain in Chile. They expect to have it up and running by 2018. Even though it's stuck here on earth, it will have enormous mirrors expected to provide images fifteen times sharper than the Hubble, which are already pretty darn good. Some think it will be powerful enough to be able to image planets far beyond our solar system.

Web Search Keywords

| *milky way bar* | *milky way galaxy* | *james maxwell* | *electricity and magnetism* | *spiral galaxies* |

Chapter 6

Why Can't We Ever Just Sit Still?

"Can't you just sit still, even for a minute?" Did your parents ever ask anything like that? Mine sure did. And plenty.

As you read in the previous chapter, there's a lot of motion going on in the universe, but when you sit in a quiet room and look around, there doesn't seem to be all that much going on. Or is there?

We're fortunate to live on our little planet, the third stone from the sun. It spins around once every day and also revolves around the sun once a year. The sun in turn revolves around the center of the galaxy once every 250 million years or so, which is moving too. When you add that all up, we're all moving around a lot faster than you might ever imagine.

> "You can get help from teachers, but you are going to have to learn a lot by yourself, sitting alone in a room."
> *Dr. Seuss*

How fast?

The fastest runners on the planet used to dream about breaking the four-minute mile, meaning that they could run one mile in less than four minutes. To do that, you'd have to run at a speed of at least fifteen miles per hour (mph). Roger Bannister was the first man to conquer the four-minute mile by running it in 3:59.4 in 1954.

Hicham El Gurrouj of Morocco gained the current record when he pared the time down to 3:43.13 in 1999, for a speed of slightly more than 16 mph.

Most people typically walk, jog, or skip at around five miles per hour. That means if you do your thing for one hour, you'd cover five miles, unless you got tired after forty-five minutes and slowed down.

You probably drive on the interstate at around 60 mph, unless you don't mind getting a speeding ticket. That translates to about 100 kilometers per hour. Going at 60 mph is four times faster than Roger. It covers a mile a minute, and is much easier on the legs, especially if you want to cover the full sixty miles.

Jet airliners are obviously faster still and generally cruise at around 500 mph. Of course, that's why it's a lot faster to fly from New York to Miami than it is to drive there. And it's way faster than walking—about 100 times faster, in fact. Jets are faster than cars, and cars are faster than legs. Big deal.

Let's put the pedal to the metal and go faster.

Breaking the speed of sound turned out to be a bigger deal than breaking the four-minute mile. The speed that sound travels in air varies, depending on factors like temperature, pressure, density, and humidity. Sound travels at 768 mph in dry air, at 20°C (68°F). The speed of sound is usually quoted in *Mach* numbers, which take into account local atmospheric conditions. Mach one is a benchmark number and means you're traveling at exactly the speed of sound under the conditions you're currently in.

The first *official* record of supersonic flight took place October 14, 1947, about seven years before Roger's famous mile. Chuck Yeager piloted Glamorous Glennis, a rocket-powered Bell XS-1, through the sound barrier, although there had been many unsupported claims of supersonic flight for years. Exactly fifty years and one day later (October 15, 1997), Andy Green put it to the floor and drove the ThrustSSC

> "And now my friend, the first-a rule of Italian driving. [*Franco rips off his rear-view mirror and throws it out of the window.*] What's-a behind me is not important."
> *Gumball Rally*

(SSC is for Super Sonic Car) faster than the speed of sound. What? In a car? There's no need for a rear-view mirror when you're driving that fast.

When a plane travels through the air, it has to push air out of its way. That produces two pressure waves that travel at the speed of sound. One is ahead of the plane and the other behind. At the speed of sound, the two waves become very compressed. To go faster, the plane has to break through the front wave, leaving both waves behind. When the two waves collide, they create a clap like the sound of thunder. You can actually make your own sonic boom with a surprisingly simple piece of equipment. If you know any cowboys, borrow a bullwhip. When you crack it, the sound is actually a tiny sonic boom because the end of the whip is moving faster than the speed of sound.

Sonic booms may well have been going on much longer than we've been around. Apatosaurus (sometimes also called brontosaurus, and enjoyed by Fred Flintstone in "Brontoburgers") lived during the Jurassic period, about 150 million years ago. I think I even spotted a bunch of them in the film *Jurassic Park*. They were big critters, measuring seventy-five feet in length and weighing in at around twenty-five tons. In the May 1997 issue of *Discover Magazine*, an article proposed that when these great beasties whipped their tails, they could have generated sonic booms. Computer models suggest that the sound would have resembled the firing of large cannons. Perhaps that could have been used to scare off predators (or maybe sometimes attracting some of the nastier ones). On the other hand, it could have been just how they kept track of each other. At any rate, getting hit by a supersonic tail would definitely hurt.

Bullets travel at around 1,000 mph. That makes Superman pretty cool, because he's supposed to be faster than a speeding bullet.

A fast jet fighter can get up to about 2,000 mph. But not above your house, I hope, because the shockwave that follows it might smash some of your windows.

The space shuttle travelled at more than 15,000 mph to stay in orbit. That was before the fleet was retired from service in July 2011.

If you were to drive from New York City to Miami, you'd travel 1,288 miles. One question worth asking besides, "Are we there yet?" is "What's up with the funky 1,288-mile number?" You should always be on the lookout for what some call *bogus accuracy.* This over-exact distance of 1,288 miles, which I took from a travel website, depends entirely on what part of New York you leave from and what part of Miami you're heading to, not to mention any detours you might have to make along the way. Anytime someone gives you an over-exact number like that, it's always good to question it. So let's just call it 1,200 miles. Traveling that distance at 60 mph should take you twenty hours, or the better part of a day, to get there, not counting bathroom breaks. At the space shuttle's orbit speed of 15,000 mph, it would only be a five-minute trip, ignoring early arrival for check-in and security line-ups.

However, none of this is really anything compared to what's going on all around us all the time. So take your seats and buckle up.

The earth rotates on its axis every day, giving rise to night and day. The earth is a pretty big place, so the middle bit has to cover a lot of ground in order to spin around each day. In fact, you'd be travelling a little more than 1,000 miles per hour if you were anywhere near the equator. I like to think that anyone standing, or more likely lying, on a beach down south is a kind of Superman, Superwoman, or Supergirl. They'd be traveling as fast as a speeding bullet and probably getting a great suntan while they're at it.

"It's a small world but I wouldn't want to paint it."
Steven Wright

If you were on the north pole, you'd just be spinning—not really covering any distance at all. But who wants to live on the north pole anyway?

There's much more going on with the earth than just spinning because it also travels around the sun once a year. That's why we have seasons. Because earth is far away from the sun, about ninety-three million miles, in fact, it has to move pretty fast to make its 600 million-mile annual round trip. It turns out that the earth is moving at about 60,000 mph, just to get us around the sun that one time each year. At that speed, you could make it from Miami to New York in about one minute.

The sun isn't exactly standing still, either. It rotates around the center of our galaxy, and we all get dragged along. Galaxies are collections of billions of stars, many like the sun. Some are bigger, some smaller, some hotter, and some cooler. Many have planetary systems of their own, and new planets around distant stars are being discovered every day. Stars in galaxies are all a lot farther apart than we are from the sun. Because these distances are so gigantic, the sun has to travel at about 450,000 mph just to keep pace rotating around the center of the galaxy, and hold onto its place in our cosmic neighborhood.

More astonishingly, there are billions of far-away galaxies out there, and many are similar to our own. If you're beginning to get the idea that the universe is a pretty big place and everything in it is far apart, then you're absolutely on the right track. But there's even more because all the galaxies in the universe are moving apart from each other at astonishing speeds.

When you add it all up, just sitting in that chair in your quiet room, it's estimated that you are moving, or should I say racing, across the universe at roughly 1.3 million miles per hour!

Remember that twenty-hour car ride to Miami? You'll have covered that distance in the time it takes you to finish this sentence. That's hardly enough time for an in-flight movie, let alone a meal, unless you're a really fast eater and get fast in-flight service.

So if anyone ever says: "Can't you just sit still, even for a minute?" you can confidently reply: "No. And neither can you."

Web Search Keywords

| *space shuttle* | *galaxies* | *superman* | *faster than a speeding bullet* | *four minute mile, roger banister*| *speed record car* | *speed record boat* | *speed record plane* | *speed of sound* | *breaking sound barrier* |

Chapter 7

How Fast is Fast?

About a hundred years ago, a remarkable young man named Albert Einstein came up with ideas that completely changed the way we look at the world.

Some of his ideas eventually gave rise to many of the technologies that we enjoy today, like CDs, flat-screen TVs, digital cameras, and even GPS devices. Then again, some science snobs have been known to say, "The microwave oven is the consolation prize in our struggle to understand physics."

> "The science of today is the technology of tomorrow."
> *Edward Teller*

Many of Einstein's discoveries came from one seemingly simple idea; although it wasn't at all obvious at the time. He imagined that there is a cosmic speed limit in the universe. In a way, it's like how you aren't supposed to drive faster than sixty miles per hour on a highway. But the universal speed limit isn't a guideline, where you could cheat a bit and go faster as long as you don't mind getting a speeding ticket. Instead, Albert's idea was that an *absolute* speed limit exists in nature. It's a law that can never be broken, even if you're prepared to pay a million-dollar fine. Nothing can go faster. Not even if you've got the biggest, hottest spaceship, with chrome hubs, tons of underglow lighting, and a wicked stereo system.

Einstein figured that the speed limit of the universe is exactly the speed that light travels at, not surprisingly called the speed of light. And all this came simply from asking himself questions about the nature of light.

The speed of light is astonishingly fast.

It is almost inconceivable, clocking in at 186,282 miles per *second.* That works out to be about 670 million mph or about 130 million times faster than you can walk or jog, even with a brand new pair of Nikes on. At this breakneck speed, light from the sun takes only about eight minutes to get here, and remember it's coming from ninety-three million miles away. In your car, a trip from the sun to the earth would take about 177 years, not counting any bathroom breaks. That wouldn't likely slow you down too much though, because there aren't many truck stops along the way.

> "OK, so what's the speed of dark?"
> *Steven Wright*

Remember that car trip from New York to Miami? How'd you like to make it back in less than a thousandth of a second? Think about that next time you switch on your bedroom light.

A lot of people might think that electrons travel down a wire at somewhere near the speed of light. The reasoning is that when you flip the switch, the bulb goes on instantaneously, so the electrons in the wire must at least be moving very fast. It is true that any signal in a wire, like flipping a switch or talking on a telephone, travels near the speed of light. That's because it's the combined result of the movements of all the electrons along the length of the wire. In a simplistic way, it's a bit like turning on a full garden hose compared to an empty one.

If you were to ask: "How fast does any *individual* electron move when it goes down a wire?" you'd get a different answer. While it's true that the electrons themselves are all moving at extreme speeds inside the wire, they move in all directions and are constantly changing from up to down, forwards, backwards, and side to side.

It turns out that despite all their frantic movement, each electron is, on average, just drifting along down the wire. They drift at a snail's pace, roughly about three or four inches in an hour.

But do not underestimate the little snail. The first *Guinness Gastropod Championship* was held in 1999 in the O'Conor Don Pub in Central London. It featured an attempt to break the world thirteen-inch sprint record, currently held by Archie (1995), at two minutes and twenty seconds. That works out to roughly ten times faster than our supposedly speedy electron. Snail racing is popular primarily in the United Kingdom, and races start with the announcement: "Ready. Steady. Slow!"

> "Time and patience would bring the snail to Jerusalem."
> *Irish Proverb*

Something new came up about the speed of light in late 2011. The results of an experiment suggested that it might actually be possible to travel faster than the speed of light after all. Scientists at the CERN laboratory in Geneva studied tiny particles called neutrinos (pronounced "new-*tree*-nose") that have fascinated people for a long time. The curious thing about them is that they don't really mess around with stuff. They just pass on by, like stray cats. It has been estimated that on earth there are around sixty-five billion of these little guys passing through every square centimeter of us every second. When I measure my torso, that would add up to more than 200 trillion of them going through me every second. Most of them pass through the earth and come out the other side, completely unscathed.

> "No amount of experimentation can ever prove me right; a single experiment can prove me wrong."
> *Albert Einstein*

What scientists at CERN have claimed is that neutrinos can actually travel faster than the speed of light, which would upset a century of thinking and raise all sorts of questions. There are skeptics, however. You always need to perform many experiments to prove anything. In the words of Stephen Hawking, "It is premature to comment on this. Further experiments and clarifications are needed." So we'll just have to wait and see. To put the results of their experiment in the context of our day-to-day lives, which I always like to do, here's what it means.

You read earlier that the speed of light is about 186,282 miles per second. According to the experiment, the neutrinos appear to have travelled at 186,286 miles per second.

Let's say we were to race from Ney York to Los Angeles, like in the film *The Gumball Rally*, and I was driving a brand new Ferrari 458 with a top speed of 201 mph. In your 458n (the "n" being for the neutrino version) you would hit 201.004 mph. The trip is about 2,400 miles, so in our race across America, the 458n would arrive just about one second earlier (or eighteen car-lengths).

Web Search Keywords

| *speed of light* | *millennium falcon jumps to light speed* | *faster than the speed of light*|

Chapter 8,000,000,000

How Big Is Big?

"As long as you're going to be thinking anyway, think big."
—*Donald Trump, The Donald*

Think about big numbers—really big numbers.

One million is just a number, like one, two, ten, one hundred, or even one thousand. It's a thousand thousand. The idea of one million used to be about as big as anyone could ever conceive, having been introduced only as recently as the thirteenth century. While that might sound like a long time ago, it really isn't when you consider that mathematics had been around at least three thousand years before that. Bigger still, one billion is one thousand million. Even bigger, one trillion is one thousand billion. Just add three zeroes to a billion and stir. And hey, what's a billion between friends?

"If I had a million dollars, I'd be rich."
The Barenaked Ladies

The names of even bigger numbers, each representing one thousand of each previously named big number, run like this: million, billion, trillion, quadrillion, quintillion, sextillion, septillion, octillion, nonillion, and dectillion. The list goes on and on. That's in the United States, the UK, and other countries that have adopted the *short scale* of naming large numbers. Oddly enough, in other countries, including certain parts of Europe and India, the use of the *long scale* is preferred, where the same names represent completely different numbers. That can be pretty confusing.

To cut down on confusion and simplify arithmetic, many people and, not surprisingly, most scientists use *scientific notation.* It's based on a ten with a numeric superscript. For example, one million would be written as 10^6 and represents a one followed by six zeroes (1,000,000). To illustrate the confusion of not using scientific notation, one trillion in the US short scale is 10^{12}, whereas under the long scale, one trillion would mean 10^{18}. It also simplifies matters when I can say ten to the fifty-seventh, rather than having to know that it would otherwise be classified as an octodecillion, at least in the United States.

Everything is big in this universe (and I say *this* universe because there might well be many more out there); distances to stars or galaxies are measured in millions and billions or even trillions of miles. So it's worthwhile to try to get a good grasp on what these gigantic numbers really mean by trying to visualize them.

If you were to measure the thickness of an American penny, you'd find that it's about 0.061 inches, or just over six hundredths of an inch thick. To stack pennies all the way to the moon, which is about 240,000 miles away, or roughly 200 round trips between New York and Miami, it would take about 250 billion pennies, worth about $2.5 billion and would weigh 700,000 tons. By comparison, the total cost of the Apollo space program was $25.4 billion for the six manned visits to the moon (as presented to US Congress in 1973).

"That's one small step for [a] man, one giant leap for mankind."
—*Neil Armstrong*

The missing "a" in that quote caused some debate at the time. While Neil's statement had been carefully scripted, you couldn't hear it in the broadcast and its omission changed the meaning of this most historic quote. After considerable analysis over many years,

Neil is reported to in fact have said "*a* man." But when I listen to it, I'm still not entirely convinced. You can hear it for yourself on YouTube.

When it comes to stacking pennies to the moon, while I usually have lots of loose change kicking around in my desk drawer, it's not quite enough to get there. There is a fun story, however, about collecting pennies. It starts with the company Coinstar that cashes loose change, which is a cool idea in itself. It's been around for a couple of decades and over the years has exchanged more than 350 billion coins. You may have seen or even used one of their kiosks, which look like big vending machines. The idea is that you throw your loose change into the machine and it counts it up. It gives you a receipt that you can exchange for bills, credit card advances, or bank transfers. Naturally, Coinstar keeps track of all their transactions, the average of which is reported to be roughly thirty-eight dollars. Based on this, they estimate that there is about $10.5 billion stashed away in the desk drawers of American households right now.

The record-holder for penny exchanging is Edmond Knowles who deposited 1,308,549 pennies in 2005, worth about $13,000. He stored them in four oil drums and when he delivered them, they weighed more than 4.5 tons. It took more than seven hours to count, but thirty-eight years to collect. Benjamin Franklin said, "A penny saved is a penny earned." Then again, a penny saved is just a penny, unless you're Edmond, I guess.

Let's paint the picture of one billion dollars a different way. If you earned a minimum wage of $7.25 per hour with a 40-hour workweek, it would take sixty-six years to earn $1 million, or sixty-six thousand years to earn one billion dollars. By comparison, Homo sapiens (Latin, for "knowing man") are thought to have first appeared on the planet more than 200,000 years ago, although modern humans have only been around for the past 50,000 years. Talk about a life savings.

Remember the speed of light?

Because the universe is so vast—and inches, feet, miles, or even millions of miles are miniscule by comparison—astronomers often prefer to use different measures of distance. One of these is known as a *light year*, the distance that light travels in one year. Because the speed of light is so fast, one light year turns out to be a gigantic distance, being about six trillion miles! One trillion miles is 1,000 billion miles, and that is one colossal number.

The closest star to earth (*besides* the sun—yes I know the trick question) is Proxima Centauri. (*Proxima* is Latin for *close to.*) It's believed to be part of a three-star system that includes the binary Alpha Centauri (A and B), previously thought to be our nearest neighbor. Our next-door neighbor is a red dwarf. It's pretty small, dim and rather boring. Red dwarfs are usually less than half the size of the sun, which itself is pretty modestly sized. You can't even see it without a powerful telescope. One curious aspect of it is that if you could pick up a cup full of its "stuff," it would weigh roughly forty times as much as what makes up the sun. So maybe it's more of a *fat* red dwarf.

Our next-door neighbor isn't exactly just across the street. It happens to be about 4.2 light years away. That turns out to be about twenty-five trillion miles, which anybody would call a bit of a hike. To drive there in a car at 60 mph, it would take you about forty-seven million years. In a Toyota Prius, which has great gas mileage of about seventy miles per gallon, that trip would take 360 billion gallons of fuel. Based on current global oil production rates, the trip would require roughly 3,000 years of production. And remember that production rates are about to, or have already started to decline. One good question to ask is how much gasoline do you actually get out of a barrel of oil? It turns out to be only about 30 percent, so my 3,000-year calculation should be more like 10,000 years. I think the world would be pretty pissed off to go without oil for the next 10,000 years (which would be the year 12,012, well past the *Star Trek* generation).

The furthest-away object ever seen to date is called *GRB 090423*, a name that doesn't exactly roll off the tongue. It's not so much an object, as it was a burst of energy that arrived here as gamma rays, which are like high-powered x-rays. The burst arrived on April 23, 2009, and lasted only about ten seconds. It's believed to be the result of the formation of a black hole, which you'll read about in a later chapter. The flash took place about thirteen billion light years away, when the universe was only a baby, about 200 to 400 million years young. If you live to be eighty years old, that would be like you at fifteen months. Any time we look up at far-away objects, it's a bit like opening up a time capsule because it took so long for the light to arrive.

Astronomers have other big measuring sticks besides the light year.

One *astronomical unit* is the average distance between the earth and the sun. It's averaged because the earth's orbit around the sun is not a perfect circle. It's an ellipse.

Another is the *parsec.* That stands for the *par*allax of one *sec*ond of an angular degree. That might sound complicated, but it really isn't. You can see parallax for yourself if you stand in front of a post or a tree and look at an object directly behind it. It appears to move when you move from side to side. Instead, you can extend your arm and point your thumb at the moon the way Tom Hanks did in the film *Apollo 13*. Alternate closing each eye, and the moon appears to move. The open eye where it doesn't move, compared to having both eyes open, is your dominant eye.

> "Houston, we have a problem."
> *Commander Jim Lovell, Apollo 13*

If you look at a particular star and then look at it again six months later, when the earth is on the opposite side of the sun, the star appears to move against distant stars behind it. This is one way that astronomers estimate the distances to stars. A parsec turns out to roughly 3.26 light years. The term shows up in the film *Star Wars*, when Han Solo claims the Millennium Falcon made the "Kessel Run" in less than twelve parsecs. That's very odd given that the parsec is a measure of distance, not time, although it stirred much debate among science fiction buffs over what Han actually meant by the quote.

We live in a pretty big neighborhood, and that's the reason why we need big measuring sticks. There will always be plenty to imagine and lots of questions to ask the next time you look toward the stars.

We've seen lots of big numbers, so now might be a good time to ask: "What's the biggest number?"

That's a bit of a tough one. People started asking it a long time ago and have kept on asking it over the years. If you start with the number *one*, you can always keep adding one more "1" to it. So the biggest number turns out to be more of a concept than an actual number. It's something that goes on and on forever, called *infinity*, and usually is written as a sideways eight: ∞. The idea of infinity comes up in math and science all the time. Mathematically, infinity is the result you get by dividing any number by zero (except zero divided by zero, which is indeterminate and not really a number at all).

"Two things are infinite: the universe and human stupidity; and I'm not sure about the universe."
Albert Einstein

The craziest thing about infinity is that it comes in different forms. If you were to count in integers (one, two, three, four …) it's called a *countable infinity*. But there are other kinds of numbers, like the real numbers that represent fractions. There are an infinite number of real numbers just between zero and one. Counting the real numbers is classified as an uncountable infinity. And there are more. Georg Cantor, a German mathematician who lived in the 1800s, came up the idea that there are, in fact, an infinity of infinities. Weird huh?

While there are lots of enormous named numbers, there are a couple that some people talk about. One example is a *googol*, which is not to be confused with Google, although it probably inspired the company name. Milton Sirotta coined the name googol in 1938, when he was nine. His uncle, mathematician Edward Kasner, formally defined a googol as 10^{100}, which is a one followed by 100 zeroes. Written out it looks like this:

10,000,000,000,000,000,000,000,000,000,000,000,
000,000,000,000,000,000,000,000,000,000,000,00
0,000,000,000,000,000,000,000,000,000,000

If you were to count it out in the usual way that people try to measure seconds by counting, "One Mississippi, two Mississippi," and so on, even if you'd started counting at the beginning of time, you'd have barely put a scratch in a googol because the age of the universe in seconds is only about $4x10^{17}$ (a four followed by seventeen zeroes).

It has an even bigger brother, dubbed a *googolplex*, which is a one followed by a googol of zeroes. Little Milton gets credit for this one too and described it as writing zeroes until you got tired. Astronomer and TV personality Carl Sagan calculated that to write out a googolplex of digits on paper with a typewriter, it would occupy more space than the known universe.

"She's one in a million, she's one in a billion, she's one in a googolplex."
Back to the Future

Like stacking pennies to the moon, stacking pennies all the way to edge of the observable universe, which is believed to be forty-six or forty-seven billion light years away, would take roughly $3x10^{29}$ pennies (or a three followed by twenty-nine zeroes). That's still nothing compared to a mere googol, let alone a googolplex.

There are many even bigger numbers used in mathematics, but these two seem big enough to me.

Enough about numbers: The longest non-technical or non-coined word in the English language is *antidisestablishmentarianism* (twenty-eight letters). It describes a political movement in 1860s Britain opposed to the disestablishment or separation of church and state. Twenty-eight is not exactly a googol, but it's pretty big word nevertheless. One long coined word is *hippopotomonstrosesquipedaliophobia* (thirty-five letters) and ironically refers to the fear of long words.

Web Search Keywords
| *infinity* | *grb090423* | *biggest number* | *googol* | *googolplex* | *all the way to the moon honeymooners* | *size of the universe* | *gamma ray bursts* | *carl sagan* |

Chapter 9

A Paradox in the Game of Baseball

"Beisbol, been berry, berry good to me!"
—*Chico Escuela, Saturday Night Live*

I've always admired the Ancient Greek thinkers—not only because they imagined and asked so much about the world and the stars, but also because they loved to explore paradoxes.

Paradoxes come in many forms. They are like puzzles or riddles that make you think, "How could that possibly be true?" when there doesn't seem to be any simple explanation as to why not. Paradoxes make you think.

The Ancient Greek philosopher Zeno was one particularly paradoxical fellow. He posed more than forty paradoxes, but sadly, only nine have survived. They were described as being immeasurably subtle and profound. The story of his life is known only through the writings of the likes of Plato and Socrates. He was described as being skilled at arguing both sides of any question, and was regarded by many as the universal critic. He has been credited with the *concept* of the number zero, in contrast to just using zero as a placeholder. The ancient Mayans and possibly the Indian mathematician and astronomer Aryabhata had already thought of zero that way. If Zeno did have anything to do with zero, even in at least popularizing the idea, maybe it got misspelled somewhere along the way. He is also reputed to be one of the first great thinkers to propose the concept of infinity. If any of this is true, I guess he had both ends of the number spectrum covered.

Some of his best paradoxes were similar because they often depended on interpreting the idea of infinity and the meaning of zero. The Ancient Greeks were not quite sure about all that. What they asked about zero was: "How can nothing be something?"

My version of one of his best paradoxes involves baseball. I call it the *baseball paradox*, and I think it's funny that it's based on a question asked thousands of years before the great game of baseball was conceived.

If I throw a baseball at you, and it gets halfway to you, it still has halfway to go again and again before it hits you, right? So, my million-dollar question to every multi-million-dollar-a-year professional baseball player out there is simply this: "How can the ball ever actually hit you if it always keeps having halfway to go again?" What makes the question interesting and paradoxical is that we all instinctively know that if you don't duck, you'll probably take it in the ear.

> "Heeey batter, batter, batter, batter. Swing batter."
> *Ferris Bueller's Day Off*

These kinds of dilemmas and paradoxes are based on infinite processes and gave a lot of people headaches for a long time. Too bad there wasn't any Advil back then. Questions about these kinds of paradoxes continued to be the subject of debate in mathematics and philosophy for many years. Some went unresolved for thousands of years.

Any question that you have to think about for a long time makes it, to borrow the words of Chico, a "berry, berry good" question. Keep asking questions. They make people think, and make *you* think too!

There's a fun paradox known as the liar's paradox, credited to Eubulides in the fourth century BC. He was best known for his seven paradoxes. It even appears in a *Star Trek* episode ("I, Mudd").

It isn't important to know the entire plot of the episode other than knowing it takes place on a planet inhabited by androids and ruled by a human named Harcourt Fenton "Harry" Mudd. He wants to get off the planet, but the androids worship him and won't let him leave. In their attempt to escape, Harry and Captain Kirk, who somehow ended up on the planet, pose a dilemma to Norman, the chief android.

> "This isn't all that true."
> *Steven Wright*

Kirk says: "Everything Harry Mudd says is a lie." Then Harry adds, "I am telling a lie." If everything Harry says is a lie, and if he says he's lying, then he must be telling the truth. But that is impossible because he always lies. When Norman tries to resolve this self-contradictory and circular logical loop, the android short-circuits and burns out. It's silly, but makes for a pretty entertaining episode.

Here are a few more examples of paradoxes that might get you thinking:

- What happens when Pinocchio says: "My nose will be growing?"
- All I know is that I know nothing at all.
- Everybody lies.
- If this sentence is not true, then Santa Claus exists.

Web Search Keywords
| *paradoxes* | *star trek liars paradox* | *zenos paradoxes* | *chico escuela snl video* | *list of paradoxes* |

Chapter 10

A Good Question to Ask Ketchup

Let's put aside all the far-out and far-away space and math stuff and talk about ketchup—just plain old ketchup. Most people love ketchup, but it also turns out that there's some really cool science going on in that bottle too.

The biggest ketchup manufacturer is undoubtedly Heinz, which has been producing it since 1867. Heinz sells about 650 million bottles a year, plus the equivalent of two single serving packets for every man, woman, and child on the planet (by my count that's about another 20 percent more). The bottles alone are enough to fill eighty-five Olympic-size swimming pools.

> "To do a common thing uncommonly well brings success."
> *H. J. Heinz*

The label says "57 Varieties," which is their company slogan. Today, Heinz has more than 5,700 varieties. It turns out that the original fifty-seven were inspired by the lucky numbers of owner Henry James Heinz and his wife. The idea of luck is something that we'll save for another chapter.

It's good to ask questions about everything, even things as seemingly simple as ketchup. There's more to ketchup than merely tomato sauce mixed with vinegar, flavors, and sugar, and it illustrates how interesting ideas are around us all the time.

If ketchup could speak, what would you ask it? Don't ask it, "When were you invented?" or "What you are made from?" That would amount to nothing but boring small talk. Instead, you might well ask ketchup: "Hey, why do I have to shake up the bottle to get anything out of you?" Some people, like the character George in *Seinfeld,* prefer to bang on the end of the bottle, which seems to work pretty well too.

"Information is not knowledge."
Albert Einstein

The ketchup bottlers of the world have stolen some of the story here—most bottles that you buy from grocery stores these days are squeezable. They are depriving inquiring minds of interesting questions to ask. Thankfully, you can still find ketchup in old-fashioned glass bottles in many restaurants and just about every diner. The idea of squeezable ketchup comes up in a *Seinfeld* episode ("The Kiss Hello") when Jerry has to go to his Grandmother's apartment to open a bottle of ketchup for her. George says, "You know, there's gotta be an easier way to open ketchup," to which Jerry replies, "Like toothpaste?" "Yea!"

The most interesting thing about ketchup, apart from its taste and nutritional value (as an antioxidant), lies in its physical nature. Ketchup is *thixotropic*, which is a peculiar property. Whoever came up with this ridiculous name at least got the *thix* part of it right, because ketchup is thick.

"Blood may be thicker than water, but it's certainly not as thick as ketchup. Nor does it go well with French fries."
Jarod Kintz

Ketchup is normally a gel. But when you shake it up a bit, it changes from its natural gel state into a liquid, which makes it easier to pour out of the bottle. This property is one reason why mudslides sometimes happen during earthquakes. When a quake shakes up wet clay, that phenomenon shares many of the same properties as ketchup. It can start to flow like a liquid, covering roads, or even collapsing them, and generally making one big mess. (The process is called *liquefaction.*) *Silly Putty* is another good example, as are *space pens.*

While all this may be interesting, you already know how to get ketchup out of a bottle. You just shake it up.

A more interesting question might be: "Could I reverse all this and find something that works the other way around?" The answer is yes. And the next bit is very cool, so you absolutely have to try it sometime. Don't worry, it's completely safe and not all that messy. Okay, maybe it's a bit messy.

Here's what you do: Take some powdered cornstarch and put it into a bowl or a coffee cup, about half full. Start adding water—a little at a time. Mix it with your finger, right down to the bottom of the cup. As you mix, keep adding more water. You want it to reach a consistency that's like firm mud. Finally, add just a little more water until it turns into a thick liquid.

The fun and rather bizarre part is that the result is the opposite of what happens when you shake up a bottle of ketchup. A scientist would describe what you do when you shake a ketchup bottle, as putting work into it. That causes it to change from its natural gel state into a liquid. In contrast, when you put work into your cornstarch mixture, it thickens up.

The best way to play with this mess is to jab your index finger into the middle of the bowl. To your surprise, it will solidify on impact and then release back into a semi-liquid. You can even plunge your fingers into it and pull out a chunk from the bowl. As you pull it up, it melts away because you're no longer putting work into the mixture. That's the potentially messy bit. The first time I tried this, I was spellbound.

This property of "reverse ketchup" is called *antithixotropism* by some. While that's not exactly correct, it's close enough for now. The cornstarch mixture is technically considered to be a dilatant fluid, which is much easier to say anyway. But hey, what's in a name? You might also wonder about mustard.

> "Mustard's no good without roast beef."
> *Chico Marx*

It's always good to ask questions—even about things as simple as ketchup.

Do yourself a favor and look up "Pool filled with non-Newtonian fluid" on YouTube. It looks like more fun than just using a coffee mug.

Web Search Keywords

| *ketchup* | *57 varieties* | *nutritional value of ketchup* | *mustard non-newtonian fluid* | *cornstarch and water mixture experiment* | *anticipation ketchup ad* | *ketchup recipe* |

Chapter 11

How to Surf the North Pole

"Let's go surfin' now, everybody's learning
how, come on a safari with me"
—*The Beach Boys, Surfin' Safari*

Who doesn't love skating? I'd bet you'd love it even if you live in Florida and have never seen a frozen pond.

. For something as seemingly simple as frozen water, ice turns out to be one tricky and mysterious solid. Some of its properties are still the subject of scientific debate.

How do skates work?

The standard textbook answer is that they melt a thin layer of ice under the blade that lets you glide over the surface. The idea is that even if you don't weigh all that much, the pressure of your weight concentrated onto your skinny blades translates into enough pressure to melt the ice under you. So when you skate, it's as if you're surfing. That seems way cooler than skating and a whole lot warmer at the same time.

"In skating over thin ice, our safety is in our speed."
Ralph Emerson Waldo

"Surfing is out of this world. You can't imagine the thrill of shooting the curl. It positively surpasses every living emotion I've ever had."
—*Gidget*

The idea of blades melting the ice turns out to be *old-school* thinking. Opponents argue that the concentrated pressure from your blades isn't nearly enough to melt the ice in any meaningful way. Others counter by claiming that it's the friction between your skates and the ice that melts it. One thing I can tell you from experience is that I don't need a pair of skates to melt ice and glide. Give me an iced-up sidewalk and a pair of size eleven brogues and I'm entirely capable of taking one huge wipeout.

Why is ice so slippery then? Could it be that the surface of ice is always a bit liquid, even at temperatures well below freezing?

Michael Faraday figured it out more than one hundred years ago. He was a great physicist and chemist who lived in the 1800s. Albert Einstein admired him greatly, and always kept a photograph of Faraday in his study (along with Newton and Maxwell). As far as I'm concerned, if your photo was hanging on Albert's wall, you were a big shot. Faraday contributed enormously to our understanding of electricity and magnetism, among many other fields, but he was also interested in the nature of ice.

Do you think you can stick two ice cubes together?

Faraday devised an incredibly simple experiment to help him understand the nature of ice, one that you can try for yourself. All you need to do is open a freezer door. People might think that ice cubes are slippery because the heat from our fingers or the temperature of the room melts them. However, if you take two cubes and squeeze them together for about ten seconds, they actually stick to each other. Faraday's idea was that the two surfaces fuse together in the same way that all the crystals on the inside bond with each other in solid ice. Ice likes to live in a hexagonal crystal shape. That is why snowflakes have six sides. Everything is very orderly on the inside of ice cubes, but at the surface, there's nothing to hold the outside layer of the ice inside, so it's always a bit wet on the outside. By fusing the cubes together, what was the outside becomes the inside.

Incidentally, Faraday also invented the Bunsen burner. I wonder if he ever used one to watch ice melt?

I always find it remarkable how much of nature that might seem simple on the surface can turn out to be much more complex once you get inside it. In the case of ice, maybe it's the other way around.

Another great question to ask about skating is this: "Can skates stop working if it gets really cold outside?" The answer is yes, although not many people know about it because you have to live someplace really cold, like the north pole, to experience it. Years ago, some friends and I were playing shinny (an ice hockey game with just sticks, skates, and a puck) on a frozen lake in northern Canada when something rather bizarre happened, and we all stopped gliding at more or less the same time. It suddenly felt like we were trying to skate on a paved driveway in Arizona. Skates *can* stop working if it gets too cold out because the ice isn't slippery anymore. The critical temperature varies because anytime Mother Nature gets involved, there are often no exact answers. Speaking from my experience, however, skates seem to stop working at around -40°F (which coincidentally is also exactly -40°C). Either way, that's chilly to say the least. It turned out to be a good time to head indoors anyway, because our feet were absolutely freezing.

There's colder stuff than ice, and it's *cooler* too. Dry ice is frozen carbon dioxide; it melts at about -56°C (-69°F). Catering companies sometimes use it when they transport frozen deserts. Colder still is liquid nitrogen, made from the most abundant gas in earth's atmosphere. When compressed, it becomes a liquid that boils at about -196°C (-321°F), which is pretty darned cold.

> "I worked in a health food store once. A guy came in and asked me, 'If I melt dry ice, can I take a bath without getting wet?'"
> *Steven Wright*

I'll always have a soft spot for liquid nitrogen. When I was a graduate student, and had access to a seemingly endless supply of the stuff, we played with it all the time. You can store it in a container like a thermos, and we liked to plunge things like bananas into it. They freeze quickly and can actually be shattered by hitting them on a desk or just dropping them on the floor.

There was a story going around at the time that some graduate student at another university actually plunged his finger into liquid nitrogen, just for a second. He figured that the heat from his finger would create a layer of nitrogen gas and keep the liquid away from his finger as along as it wasn't in there too long. If it's true, he'd probably seen it done before. Whoever was the first person to try this stunt was very smart, very stupid, or very lucky. Perhaps the story is just an urban myth.

All this might lead you to ask: "What's the coldest temperature?" People started asking this as long ago as the 1600s, led by Robert Boyle. He knew all about gases, temperatures, and pressure. Boyle's Law is a fundamental theory in physics and chemistry. It even explains how car engines work.

The lowest temperature, or *absolute zero*, has been set at zero K, where K is for Lord Kelvin, who devised the scale of absolute temperature. Zero Kelvin is equal to -273.15°C or -459.67°F. Helium, the second lightest element after hydrogen, can be condensed into a liquid at about 4 K, and has been the source and subject of much investigation over the years in a field known as *low temperature physics*.

Most children wonder how cold it is in space. It turns out to be pretty cool, in more ways than one. The average temperature of the universe is 2.73K. Besides the fact that it's very cold, what's way cooler about it is that it's not exactly zero. The non-zero temperature comes from the cosmic background radiation, which is a remnant of when the universe began with the big bang.

The coolest thing about it is that you can actually see it for yourself. Just turn on a TV, but disconnect the cable first. The *snow* that you see on your screen is actually a result of that 2.73K cosmic background radiation.

Background radiation had been predicted in the 1940s, and fifteen years later it was discovered by accident by Andrew Penzias and Robert Wilson while performing satellite communications experiments for Bell Telephone Laboratories. They had built an extremely sensitive instrument but couldn't get rid of the pesky hiss that you just saw on your TV. At first, they thought it must be coming from a nearby city, but to their surprise it was coming from every direction. They simply asked, "Why?" and their answer was good enough to earn them the Nobel Prize.

It's always good to look at what's going on around you and to ask yourself how could it be so?

Web Search Keywords

| *how skates work* | *beach boys surfin safari* | *speed skating apolo ohno* | *ice hockey* | *bobby orr dive video* | *extreme surfing* | *big wave surfing* | *laird hamilton* | *liquid nitrogen into a swimming pool* | *frozen banana liquid nitrogen* |

Chapter 12

One Hot Question about Global Warming

Global warming and climate change are certainly hot topics.

Just about every kid has probably wondered if there's an actual pole, like a flagpole or something, on the north pole. One way or another, this question might eventually be coming to an end.

One of the most serious problems facing the planet right now is that the polar ice caps are slowly melting away because of global warming. The earth's average surface temperature has increased by about 0.8°C (1.4°F) since the early 1900s. That might not sound like much, but the concern is that much of the increase has taken place during the last thirty years.

It's widely accepted that a large part of this has resulted from mankind's contribution to greenhouse gases from burning fossil fuels and deforestation. Greenhouse gases include carbon dioxide (CO_2), methane (CH_4), water vapor, ozone, and other gases that absorb infrared radiation emitted by the earth's surface as sunlight warms it. Greenhouse gases themselves aren't as evil as they might sound to some. They play a vital role in a healthy

> "Unless someone like you cares a whole awful lot, nothing is going to get better. It's not."
> *The Lorax*

atmosphere. Without them, it's estimated that the average surface temperature of the earth would be -18°C (0°F) compared with the 15°C (59°F) that we currently enjoy. It's just that things work best when they're kept in balance.

There are, however, other explanations for climate change. These include the theories of Milutin Milanković, a civil engineer and mathematician who lived in the early 1900s. He showed how changes in the earth's orbit and tilt, which occur regularly over thousands of years, directly affect our climate.

One way or the other, the planet is definitely warming up, because some delicate balance seems to have been lost. The Intergovernmental Panel on Climate Change (IPCC) released projections in 2007 that temperatures could rise between one and three degrees Celsius by the end of the twenty-first century. In the worst case, they could even rise by six degrees.

This book isn't about climatology or any of the political and moral issues that go along with global warming. Instead, it's about asking questions, and the subject of global warming provides plenty to ask.

> "According to a new U.N. report, the global warming outlook is much worse than originally predicted. Which is pretty bad when they originally predicted it would destroy the planet."
> *Jay Leno*

Recognizing that mankind isn't exactly helping the situation, the most obvious question to ask is whether the warming is just part of a bigger cycle that is going to happen anyway—with or without us. Is the current warming perhaps just part of how our planet works?

There have been five well-established ice ages in the earth's history, with the earliest one dating back about two billion years. Snowball earth was an extreme ice age that took place about 650 million years ago, when the earth was completely covered with ice.

Many people believe that we are actually living in an ice age right now. It's known as the *Pleistocene glaciation*, and it began about 2.5 million years ago. During any ice age, the climate alternates between glacial periods, when ice is advancing, and interglacial periods, when the ice is stable or retreating. The last glacial period in our current ice age ended about ten thousand years ago, and the ice has been retreating ever since. Much more recently, a brief period of global cooling known as the *Little Ice Age* occurred between 1550 and 1850 AD. Today, there are dramatic photographs that illustrate the shrinking of glaciers over the past hundred years. Looking at these photographs alone, however, is like walking into the last sixty seconds of a two-hour movie. The melting started when the Great Lakes were being carved out about ten thousand years ago. Not much of the ice remains other than the large sheets that cover most of Antarctica, Greenland, and the many smaller glaciers found at high altitude in mountain ranges around the world. There is also the Arctic ice pack that floats on top of the Arctic Ocean.

The climate has been measured as far back as 400,000 years ago, based on deep ice samples take at Vostok station in Antarctica. The CO_2 levels show changes that move in patterns with peaks and troughs. CO_2 began to increase from a low point about 20,000 years ago and have climbed by about 50 percent since then. We are currently slightly below all-time peak levels from 125, 240, 325, and 400 million years ago. Surface temperatures have followed a similar pattern.

If we could somehow put a halt to mankind's entire effect on climate change, it might amount to no more than standing on a beach and throwing sand at an incoming tidal wave.

The idea of global warming raises an even bigger and more important question: "Why is it sometimes so unacceptable to challenge widely accepted beliefs like global warming?" Sensitive issues can easily turn into hot potatoes. This highlights one of the greatest challenges of asking hard questions: some questions just don't sit well with anybody. Why are some questions off limits? It's easy to test this for yourself with a simple statement like, "Yes the ice is melting, but maybe it's just that ice ages end when there's no ice left." See where that gets you.

"Why fit in when you were born to stand out?"
Dr. Seuss

Simple questions about touchy subjects often strike at raw nerve endings. But sometimes, the less popular the question, the better it just might be. What many people don't seem to appreciate is that when you ask challenging questions, the questions aren't meant to discredit or attack. You're just asking a question. You might recall the story of Galileo from chapter 5. He questioned whether the sun revolved around the earth and eventually proved that it worked the other way around. Galileo was charged with heresy for his ideas, all because he refused to go along with the popular views of the time.

Everyone is in favor of being environmentally friendly, and nobody wants to junk up the planet, but it's worth asking, "What is *really* going on here?" rather than just believing popular documentaries and photographs of glaciers melting over the past hundred years.

Always question anything and everything. Ask tough questions—the tougher the better. Ask unpopular ones. Ask the ones that inspire debate. As Francis Bacon said, "A sudden bold and unexpected question doth many times surprise a man and lay him open."

Just never be afraid to always ask.

Web Search Keywords

| *global warming video* | *snowball earth video* | *ice age trailer* | *antarctica photo library* | *melting ice cube* | *polar ice cap melting* | *nasa tour of the cryosphere* | *melting ice cream video* |

Chapter 13

WHY DON'T WE MAKE MATH MORE FUN?

SO FAR, WE'VE TALKED about space, speed, distance, some really big numbers, and even ketchup. Let's turn our attention to math. Mathematics is important because it is the language of science. When I was growing up, school kids used to think that math was just one big chore. I don't think things have changed much since then.

In the early 1990s, Talking Barbies were programmed to speak from a menu of recordings. One of them used to say, "Math is tough," although it's often incorrectly quoted as, "I don't like math." That particular model was discontinued, thank goodness.

We should make it a goal to find ways to make math more fun.

> "If Barbie is so popular why do I have to buy friends for her?"
> *Steven Wright*

So just how *can* we make math more fun? One answer lies in the fascinating area of math and algebra known as *recreational mathematics*. It has been around for centuries and is all about puzzles, problems, and other curiosities. Call it math for fun. In recreational mathematics, you don't usually need to know any advanced math. The puzzles and problems rely more on logic, deductive reasoning, and thinking. Just screw on your thinking cap.

One of the earliest examples of recreational mathematics is the magic square. I first learned about it in my early school days but never gave it much thought at the time. The earliest magic square dates back to 650 BC. Legend has it that a turtle emerged from the river Lo in China, following a great flood. It was found by King Yu and had a curious pattern on its shell. It's called *Lo Shu,* which means "scroll of the river Lo." Its curious pattern was based on a 3x3 square grid where the columns, rows, and diagonals all add up to fifteen.

4	9	2
3	5	7
8	1	6

In grade school, they just drop this answer on your doorstep, like I did here. The diversion in these kinds of puzzles lies in trying to figure them out on your own. In recreational mathematics, the question would be: If you start with a 3x3 grid, could you figure out how to arrange the numbers one through nine so that the rows, columns, and diagonals all add up to the same number? The original Lo Shu turns out to be a unique solution, because the only other answers are just rotations and reflections of it.

Lots of people have spent lots of time thinking about magic squares and have devised bigger and bigger ones. The trick, of course, is making them magic.

The popular Sudoku puzzle may have been partly inspired by magic squares. The game, however, is more accurately described as a special kind of 9x9 *Latin square.* These square grids date back to the Middle Ages, and as in Sudoku, each number appears only once in each column and row. Latin squares were named and studied by Leonard Euler in the 1700s. An early version of Sudoku appeared in French newspapers in the late 1800s, although the rules weren't quite the same as present day. *Dell Magazine* published the first

Sudoku game in 1979. It soon became enormously popular in Japan and later caught on all over the world. It's fun and can be addictive for some.

One of the most influential writers in recreational mathematics was Martin Gardner, who wrote the column "Mathematical Games" for the magazine *Scientific American* for twenty-five years and published more than seventy books. He celebrated the unpredictable and liked to break away from expected patterns. His April columns occasionally tried to trick readers with some kind of April Fools' Day joke. He also devoted a number of columns to debunking pseudoscience, such as ESP, and Uri Geller's bending spoons just by thinking about it. Sometimes entertainers like Criss Angel can almost make you believe this kind of thing.

"All those who believe in psycho kinesis raise my hand."
Steven Wright

Gardner had a passion for paradoxes and things like *palindromes*, which are words or sentences that read the same way backward as forward. They date back to about 100 AD. A few examples include: "Madam I'm Adam," "Racecar" and one of my personal favorites, "Norma is as selfless as I am, Ron." Some have grown to ridiculous lengths, covering 50,000 words or more, which is about the length of this book. Of course, they are all computer-generated these days. There's one (17,826 words) that starts with "A man, a plan …" and ends with "a canal, Panama!" By far the best example of palindromic writing has to be the lyrics of a song called "Bob" by Weird Al Yankovic, which is a parody of the Bob Dylan video *Subterranean Homesick Blues.* Each line in the lyrics is a palindrome, including "A Toyota's a Toyota." You can find it on YouTube.

Martin greatly appreciated Zeno's paradoxes, which you read about in chapter 9. He was an expert in the works of Lewis Carroll, who wrote *Alice's Adventures in Wonderland* and *Through the Looking Glass.* Carroll was a mathematician himself, and his books include an abundance of math puzzles and paradoxes.

One of Gardner's puzzles came as a simple question: "Why does a mirror reflect you from right to left but not upside down?"

Another of Martin's puzzles is based on the *Möbius strip*, an object that comes from an interesting topic called *topology*, the study of shapes and surfaces. To make one will cost you less than a minute of your time. You do it just by cutting a strip from a page of paper, say an inch across. If you were to loop the two ends around and tape them together, it would turn into a loop, like a bracelet or band. Instead, let's mix things up a bit and give one end a 180-degree twist before taping the ends together. You have just created a Möbius strip. The question is this: "How many sides does it have?" If you run a pen in one continuous line from where you started all the way around this funky shape, you will find that you end up back where you started from. In topology it has only one side. How strange.

"Why did the chicken cross the Möbius strip? To get to the same side."
The Big Bang Theory

Martin's puzzle asked what you'd get if you cut the strip in half. Take the strip and poke a little hole in the middle of it with scissors. Then cut it all the way around like you did when you traced a line around it with a pen. What do you think you'll end up with? It's not two Möbius strips, in case that's what you're thinking. It only takes about another thirty seconds to see for yourself, but think about what you might end up with before you start cutting.

Its bigger brother is known as the *Klein bottle*, which is the three-dimensional version. It's sometimes described as a bottle with no inside. If you cut it in half it somehow turns into a Möbius strip.

"Math was always my bad subject. I couldn't convince my teachers that many of my answers were meant ironically."
Calvin Trillin

From the world of simple arithmetic, here's one illustration of why it's fun to think more about arithmetic than we all probably do. It's a neat game, or maybe it's more of a trick. The next time you're out shopping, give this a try. It's based on simple statistics, which you should know as much about as you possibly can. The law of large numbers is quite a big deal and something that casinos all over the world make fortunes from every day. It's based on the way randomness tends to even out over time.

It works simply by rounding up or down to the nearest dollar. If something costs $1.60, you'd round it up to two dollars. If it costs $1.37, you'd call it one dollar. It's easy to add up all the ones, twos, and threes in your head. All the rounding up or down tends to average out, and you'll end up with a remarkably accurate answer, provided you buy enough groceries. If your grocery bill is eighty dollars, you'll probably end up with a guess somewhere pretty close. You can even try it without having to leave home. Just go onto any online grocery website. I picked the first fifty items on one list, and it added up to $319 in my head. The exact total was $321.65, so I was off by less than 1 percent.

See, Barbie? Math *can* be fun.

Web Search Keywords
| *adding tricks* | *adding in your head* | *math class is tough*| *weird al yankovic bob* | *mobius strip story* | *klein bottle* |

Chapter 14

Wanna Flip for It?

"Give me a coin. All right, uh … heads,
I win, tails, you lose. Right?"
—*Ralph to Ed, The Honeymooners*

I'll never forget a freshman statistics course I took along with hundreds of other students. In one of our first classes, our professor was making a point about randomness and something widely known as the *Monte Carlo fallacy*, also called the *gambler's fallacy*. In Monte Carlo, which is famous for its casino, the setting for some of the best James Bond movies ever, people wager vast amounts of money on games like roulette that are won or lost entirely on luck.

> "Gambling: The sure way of getting nothing for something."
> *Wilson Mizner*

She had everyone in the class toss coins in a series of rounds to illustrate her point about random chance. If you threw tails you'd be out, but everyone who tossed heads would advance to the next round. The interesting thing about the game is that there is about a 1 percent chance that you can actually throw six or seven heads in a row. So in a room packed with a couple of hundred students, there's a pretty good chance that even after five tosses there'd still be a handful of survivors left to fight it out.

One of the points she was trying to make was that coins have no memory. They don't know, or care, if they've landed heads or tails the last time, ten times, fifty times or even a million times in a row. Every time you flip a coin it's a brand new 50-50 proposition. Half the time you get heads, the other half you get tails.

Some people, maybe even a lot of people, think that after ten heads in a row the next toss is more likely to be a tail. That would average out the results. People who think this way are confusing random chance with the law of large numbers. Over a long enough time, you should expect to get the same number of heads as tails, and everything will *eventually* average out. But what's long enough? It might take thousands of throws to get there and there's no reason why you couldn't have an incredible run of heads or tails somewhere in the middle. There is no such thing as odds building, and casinos make loads of money from this widespread mistaken belief.

> "We'll take the house. Honey, the chances of another plane hitting this house are astronomical. It's predisastered."
> *The World According to Garp*

Dice and cards are pretty forgetful too, which makes them good games for casino owners as well. In some card games, however, some of the randomness can be taken out. This can happen in games where cards are not returned to the deck. Counting cards is a technique that lets you keep track of which cards have been played and allows you to know which cards are more or less likely to be dealt.

A famous story about unlikely streaks took place in Monte Carlo back in the summer of 1913, when the roulette wheel came up black twenty-six times in a row. You need to know that in Monte Carlo one half of the wheel has red numbers, and the other half has black, plus one green pocket ("0") where the casino wins because it's neither red nor black, although you can bet on the green pocket if you like. In Las Vegas, there are usually two green slots ("0" and "00") that earn the house about twice as much. You can think of betting on red or black in roulette as pretty close to a coin toss. (It's actually 48.6 percent in Monte Carlo because of the green, the house's edge.) People have lost millions while on a streak when they probably thought there was some kind of imbalance going on and surely red would start coming up to even things out. I'm sure that the longer the streak continued, everyone in the room put more and more down on red. If you treat roulette as a coin toss, the odds of landing thirteen blacks in a row (which was halfway through the streak) are about one in 8,000 attempts. More precisely, it's one in 11,850 if you take the green pocket into account. Although that might sound highly unlikely, it really doesn't strike me as being all that bad. The odds for twenty-six in a row, however, are about one in 140 million. But hey, the next spin could just as easily have been another black. That would have stretched it out to a one in 290 million streak. Talk about being on a roll.

Who wouldn't like to beat a casino? Sometimes it's called beating the bank. Over the years, gamblers have tried to devise strategies where you couldn't lose. One idea that was popular in eighteenth century France was called a *martingale*. People still try to use the concept to this day, even trading in futures markets. The idea is that any time you lose, you simply double your next bet and that way will ultimately be assured of winning. In a coin tossing game, or betting on red or black in roulette, if I start with a $100 bet and lose on the first round, I bet $200 next time. If I lose again, I bet $400. I will eventually win and recover all the previous losses plus win on the original bet. Although it might take a while, people believed this strategy was guaranteed to be a winner.

> "You cannot beat a roulette wheel unless you steal money from it."
> *Albert Einstein*

There is a lot of interesting mathematics and probability theory behind this concept, sometimes referred to as *gambler's ruin*. The flaw in it lies in banking. If you were to hit a bad streak of losses, you can simply run out of enough money to keep doubling your

> "The quickest way to double your money is to fold it over and put it in your back pocket."
> *Will Rogers*

bets. If you had attempted this stunt in Monte Carlo in 1913 with a 100-franc initial bet, halfway through the streak you were down 409,500 francs and would have bet another 409,600 francs to stay alive. On spin twenty-six, the last one in the streak, you would have bet 3.4 billion francs, and it came up black again. If you still had the guts to keep going, your total loss stood at roughly 6.7 billion francs, and you would have bet 6.7 billion to continue. On spin twenty-seven it finally came up red. Congratulations, you just won 100 francs.

It's often helpful to put numbers like odds and outcomes in the context of our daily lives and in nature.

The estimate for your chance of being struck by lighting any year in the United States is about one in 775,000 (according to the National Weather Service), but other estimates vary depending on the time period selected and where you live. If you live to be eighty, the chance of being struck in your lifetime is about one in ten thousand, which strikes me as frighteningly likely. Champion golfer Lee Trevino has been struck twice by lightning. He once joked: "If you're caught on a golf course during a storm and are afraid of lightning, hold up a 1 iron, because not even God can hit a 1 iron." Now that most golfers play hybrid clubs, they might not quite understand that, but I'm old enough to get it.

US National Park Ranger Roy Sullivan holds the record for lightning strikes. That's a record I'm sure nobody wants to try to break. He was struck seven times during his thirty-five-year career. The odds of being struck just once in thirty-five years would be roughly one in 22,000. Being hit seven times works out to a chance of roughly three in one followed by thirty zeroes. This isn't entirely accurate because any time you get struck, you have a pretty good (or should I say pretty bad?) chance that you will be killed and won't be around to extend your unfortunate streak. The odds of death from a lightning strike are estimated at 10 percent. On the other hand, Roy's odds of being struck were likely increased because he worked in a park and was probably surrounded by trees most of the time.

There is an easy way to figure out how streaks work in coin tossing, even if you don't know anything about probability or want to deal with formulas. It comes with just a bit of thought.

It's easy to illustrate streaks using binary numbers, which are quite simple, but you'll need to understand them first. *Binary numbers* are *base-2* numbers, the number system on which computers work. Our natural counting system is known as *base-10*. Some say it most likely arose because we have ten fingers to count with. Maybe it could have been base-8 instead, if we'd ignored thumbs. The digits in our base-10 system are zero through nine. The next number after nine is ten, of course, being a one followed by a zero placeholder. If you keep on counting after nineteen, you wind up with a two, followed by a zero placeholder. Binary numbers work exactly the same way, but there are only ones and zeros to count with. So it's a bit like counting with your fists instead of your fingers. There isn't a *two* digit in binary, so when your count gets to two, as in zero, one, two, you have to carry a one the same way that it works in our normal counting system, giving you one and a zero (*one zero*, not to be confused with ten). With two hands, we can only count to three with our fists.

Counting in binary goes like this: 0, 1, 10, 11, 100, 101, 110, 111, 1000, and so on.

With just one hand, you could actually count to, or at least represent, thirty-one using just five fingers, as long as you can bend them like Spock. With two hands, you can get to 1023 in our natural number system. And if you were to take your shoes and socks off, and could manipulate your toes as well as Spock can move his fingers, then you could actually count in binary to 1,048,575. The way I count it, the number *four* on one hand is considered to be a rude gesture in many cultures. And you should always bring an eighteen along with you if you're going to a heavy metal concert, unless you stick your thumb out as well. In that case, it would be nineteen.

If you think of the ones as *heads* and the zeros as *tails*, just by counting in binary, you can easily figure out the chances of getting a run of heads in a coin tossing game. Counting in binary to represent the results from tossing four coins looks like this:

> 0000 (four tails), 0001, 0010, 0011, 0100, 0101, 0110, 0111, 1000, 1001, 1010, 1011, 1100, 1101, 1110, 1111 (four heads).

It's easy to look at the digits and spot any runs.

- You get *at least* two heads in a row eight times out of the sixteen possible throws, for a 50 percent chance, which are as follows: 00**11**, 0**11**0, 0**111**, 10**11**, **11**00, **11**01, **111**0, **1111**.
- To get *at least* three in a row, it turns out to be only three times, or around a 20 percent chance, namely: 0**111**, **111**0, **1111**.
- There's only one four-in-a-row possibility, **1111**, representing a one-in-sixteen, or 6 percent chance.

Another popular game, particularly in Las Vegas, is the slot machine, where you put in money and pull the handle. Three wheels spin independently, and you get paid, or more likely not, based on how three symbols come up. I understand that three cherries are very good. Although the odds greatly favor the house, people love slots anyway because sometimes even a small bet can pay off millions of dollars. The record jackpot is believed to have been one in 2009, which paid $38.7 million on a three-dollar bet. Under Nevada State Law, slot machines have to pay out at least 75 percent of the coins inserted, over time. But most casinos operate closer to 95 percent, because it encourages more gambling, and casinos always prefer to take a smaller slice of a much larger pie. That way, they make more money over the long term. This shouldn't be taken to mean that if you sit at a slot machine and put a hundred dollars into it over an hour that you'll walk away with seventy-five (or ninety-five) dollars. You might walk away with nothing; you might walk away with a lot.

I took a first-year elective course in psychology. One of the most interesting ideas that I took away from it was how people's behavior can be changed through reward and punishment.

Psychologist B. F. Skinner invented the science of experimental behavior analysis. He is regarded as the most influential psychologist of the twentieth century. There's even a reference to him in the TV series *Lost*. I bet that his ideas came from asking himself one simple question: "How can behavior be changed?"

His answer was that change can come through *reinforcement*. At first he thought that there are two kinds of reinforcement: positive (reward) and negative (punishment). The number of kinds eventually grew to four:

i. Positive reinforcement (you get a reward for doing something good);
ii. Positive punishment (your mother yells at you to prevent you from doing something dangerous and potentially harmful);
iii. Negative reinforcement (something bad for you is taken away); and
iv. Negative punishment (pain is inflicted on you, including emotional and financial).

B. F. demonstrated that the most effective way to change behavior is with random positive rewards. He did this by designing an experiment with a pigeon and a seed machine, where the bird got a seed after tapping at the machine for some varied number of times. Random positive reinforcement turned out to be a runaway success.

Others went on to look at the behavior of two groups of monkeys who could push buttons to get rewards. One group always got a treat, while the other got a treat only occasionally. Random positive rewards again turned out to be highly addictive. Some stayed up all night pressing button after button.

I remembered that the last time I was in Las Vegas. It made me laugh watching all the people (or were they monkeys?) playing slot machines. Perhaps the principle of random positive rewards also partly explains why people buy lottery tickets. With them, the reward isn't entirely about winning the jackpot, though that would be nice. Most people would eventually give up spending money on tickets after not winning for years and years. The reward and the attraction with lottery tickets come from dreaming of winning.

Unfortunately, some experimenters used negative punishment on monkeys, sometimes involving electric shocks. Presumably, these were people whose parents yelled at them if they came home with a bad report card, in an attempt to spur them to better grades. Despite their disturbing aspects, these experiments led to significant increases in understanding human behavior.

"I bought a million lottery tickets and won a dollar."
Steven Wright

A more amusing monkey-based idea is called *Shakespeare's monkey* or the *infinite monkey theorem*, which is based on a paradox.

William Shakespeare lived around the year 1600 and is the greatest writer in the history of the English language. He wrote at least thirty-eight plays, the stories and themes of which have continued to be the basis of hundreds of novels and movies, even to this day.

The premise is that if you get a monkey—or better yet, a room full of monkeys—equipped with typewriters, given enough time, they could eventually write out the complete works of Shakespeare. I laugh when I try to picture that. These kinds of ideas go all the way back to the Ancient Greeks, like Zeno, who inspired the baseball paradox. The paradox lies in the fact that while it's impossible to completely rule out that the monkeys might reproduce Shakespeare, how could they really do it?

"If you had a million Shakespeares, could they type like a monkey?"
Steven Wright

Hamlet
Act I, Scene I
Elsinore. A platform before the castle.
Francisco at his post. Enter to him Bernardo.
Bernardo: Who's there?
Francisco: Nay answer me: Stand and unfold yourself.
Bernardo: Long live the King!
Francisco: Bernardo?
Bernardo: He.

To illustrate Shakespeare's Monkey with a coin tossing game, you could represent the twenty-six letters of the alphabet and a bit more, like spaces and punctuation, with five binary digits of which there are thirty-two combinations. Let's say each correct letter is represented by all ones, or tossing five heads. To get just the first three letters "Ber" in Bernardo would be like tossing fifteen heads in a row. There are about 180,000 characters in the script of *Hamlet* (including spaces, because they make it much easier to read). To type it out would be equivalent to throwing 900,000 heads in succession. That sounds like a lot, but as in the Rolling Stones hit song, our monkey has time on his side.

When some people look at streaks and other problems like it, they often assume that you have to start counting on the first throw. Just to get the first five letters of Hamlet correct straight away has a chance of about one in thirty-four million. Keep in mind, however, that a run can start anywhere. Let's illustrate the idea with a simple example. Say you needed to toss five heads in a row to win a prize. The chance of getting five heads from five coin tosses is one in thirty-two, or about a 3 percent chance. If, however, you were to toss the coin 100 times, the chance of getting a run of at least five in a row at some point grows to more than 80 percent. The more tosses you make, the closer hitting a streak turns into a sure thing, even if you need to throw 900,000 heads in a row to write *Hamlet*. Maybe it's not as hard for the monkey after all.

"This is a thousand monkeys working at a thousand typewriters. Soon they'll have written the greatest novel known to man (reading) 'It was the best of times, it was the blurst of times?' You stupid monkey!"
—*Mr. Burns, The Simpsons*

In 2003, a group of college students received a grant to perform a real-life monkey typing experiment. It involved six monkeys and a computer. They only managed to compose five pages of text, consisting mainly of the letter "s." Apparently they got tied of or bored with the whole exercise much quicker than we'd need for Shakespeare's monkey. In the end, their frustration turned into rage, and after much peeing on it, they ended up destroying the computer. It's hard to blame them, though. I think just about everyone has felt like that about computers at one time or another.

Sometimes even simple analogies, like tossing coins, can give you useful insights that might help answer your questions.

Web Search Keywords
| *coin toss* | *james bond in monte carlo* | *roulette* | *slot machine odds* | *bf skinner reinforcement* | *shakespeare monkey simulator* | *incredible lightning strike video* |

Chapter 15

THERE'S A SUCKER BORN EVERY MINUTE

WHAT COULD BE SIMPLER than tossing a coin? Provided that you don't suffer from the Monte Carlo fallacy, you know that every time you flip it's a brand new 50-50 proposition.

Penney's game questions what you think you might know about flipping coins. It was named after Walter Penney, who proposed it in 1969. The game is a contest between two players who each select a sequence of three coin-tosses (H for heads, T for tails) such as HTH. A coin is tossed repeatedly until one of their sequences appears and decides the winner. Do our choices really make any difference? After all, isn't the game just a string of 50-50 coin flips?

Let's say you pick HHH and I pick THH.

Here's the $64,000 question: Is one of us more likely to win by having their sequence come up first, and if so, by how much? Choose one of the following statements:

(a) HHH wins 60 percent of the time.
(b) THH wins 60 percent of the time.
(c) They have an equal 50 percent chance of winning.
(d) None of the above.

The correct answer is (d) and the result is spectacular: THH has a *seven*-to-one advantage over HHH and wins 87.5 percent of the time! That's better than winning a dice game if any of five out of the six faces of a die is rolled. It has to seem completely counterintuitive to just about everybody.

While it might sound tricky at first, when you think about it, there's nothing really mysterious going on. There are eight ways to throw three coins, namely: TTT, TTH, THT, THH, HTT, HTH, HHT, and HHH. Assuming the first flip isn't a head, THH will always come up first because the sequence THHH will hit a THH before an HHH. The only way HHH can win is with an HHH in the first three flips, which has only a one-in-eight chance of happening, or a seven-to-one chance against it.

If you ever want to play the game in real life, have your opponent pick his sequence first. Then announce that you can easily beat it. All you need to do is follow this simple rule:

(i) Take his second pick and reverse it.
(ii) Make that your first selection.
(iii) Tack on his first two picks after that as your second and third choices.
(iv) Ignore the third choice in his sequence.

So his HHH results in you taking THH, and you would reply to a THT with TTH. That's all there is to it. While this strategy is not guaranteed to win any individual game, the odds of winning are stacked *highly* in your favor. In the worst case, you are twice as likely to win, and in the best case it's seven times as likely, depending the sequence he chooses.

There's another version of the game using playing cards that I think should be called Modern Warfare because it's a lot like War, the classic card game often played between ten-year-old boys on long car trips. Unlike the classic version, you don't worry about the face value of the cards. You simply choose between red and black, the same way that the heads and tails game works. You take the deck and keep turning over cards and laying them out in a row until someone's sequence comes up. That counts as one point to the winner. You continue playing over and over, discarding played cards after each round, until the deck runs out. Because you're playing longer, your odds of winning the game (using the same simple strategy) increase to somewhere between 80 and 99 percent.

This kind of game is called *non-transitive* and is related to the classic game of rock-paper-scissors (RPS). Each throw in RPS has an advantage over one throw but is disadvantaged against the other. It's called non-transitive because even though rock beats scissors, and scissors beats paper, rock loses to paper. The only way to win at it is if you can somehow anticipate what the other person is about to play, which people attempt to do in contests around the world.

It's easy to make dice games based on the same idea. Here's one version, but there are many more. Take three regular dice numbered one through six, and change the numbers with a marker.

Die 1: 2,2,4,4,9,9
Die 2: 1,1,6,6,8,8
Die 3: 3,3,5,5,7,7

The faces all add to thirty, so the average roll for each die is five, and you might think it makes them equal. However, die number one will beat die two on average ten out of eighteen possible combined rolls (55.5 percent). Die two will beat die three, and die three will beat die one, exactly the same way. In non-transitive dice, even though one beats two and two beats three, die one does *not* beat die three.

Multi-billionaire Warren Buffet is said to be a big fan. As story has it, he challenged Bill Gates (his bridge partner) to a game of his non-transitory dice and offered Gates the first choice of dice. After inspecting them, Bill is alleged to have said, "I'll play, but it's okay, I'll let you choose first."

Besides non-transitive games, there are many other examples of ideas that run completely counter to intuition and seem to defy common sense. Let's say that you wrote software that can check if a lottery ticket is likely to be a winner, and it's accurate to 99.99

percent. If you get a million hits on your website and one (and only one) of them actually turns out to be a winner, what are the chances of winning if your software says it will? More than 99 percent, right? Wrong. It's actually only 1 percent. This comes out of a theory of conditional probability known as *Bayes' theorem,* from which we learn that even though your software is 99.99 percent right, it's 0.01 percent wrong and on a million tests, the false positives far outweigh that one winner.

In case you were wondering, the quote that appears as the title of this chapter is incorrectly attributed to P. T. Barnum, who was an American showman in the mid-1800s. He created the Barnum and Bailey Circus, the Greatest Show on Earth, which was later combined with Ringling Bros.

While all of this might strike you as nothing but a curiosity, it's meant to illustrate a very important point about why you should always question everything. Trust your hunches, but question them too. That way, you'll never be a sucker.

Web Search Keywords

| *scam school video* | *war card game* | *non-transitive dice* | *world rps society* | *penney's game simulation* | *cheat your friends at a fair coin toss* | *cheating at coin tossing* | *non-transitive dice to trick your friends* |

Chapter 16

Luck, Be a Lady Tonight

Frank Sinatra performed "Luck Be a Lady" frequently in Las Vegas, ironically enough. Okay, maybe it's not all that ironic. The song originally appeared in the 1950s musical *Guys and Dolls.*

Most people, in just about every culture, have at least some belief in the idea of luck or are superstitious in some way. Ask yourself the questions below.

Do you:

- ☐ believe some people are just born lucky?
- ☐ have a lucky or unlucky number?
- ☐ have a lucky symbol, charm or maybe even lucky socks?
- ☐ have something to ward off bad luck or evil?
- ☐ drive with extra care on Friday the thirteenth?
- ☐ hope you'll never break a mirror?

If you have no check marks, then you're probably fooling yourself.

But why should you or anybody believe in luck or superstition?

The idea of luck is a fun topic to explore because it seems to be a part of most of our day-to-day lives, even though some might scoff, or least pretend to scoff at the idea. One good place to start is by asking: "Where did the idea of luck come from, and why is it part of our lives?"

Luck and superstition date at least as far back as Ancient Egypt. Scarabs (a type of beetle) were considered lucky for many reasons. They were thought to pay homage to Ra, god of the sun, by rolling around in dung at sunrise. That might not sound like much of a tribute, but many believed that it coaxed the sun to pop up over the horizon at dawn each day.

> "Everything in life is luck."
> *Donald Trump, The Donald*

Luck surely appeared eons before that, when humans, who lived in caves and makeshift shelters, struggled just to survive. Early man must have relied on ideas like luck and superstition to help define the world and make some sense out of what was going on. There was just no other way to understand it.

> "We believe in luck. How else can we explain the success of those we don't like?"
> *Jean Cocteau*

Something deep inside our minds has always made mankind want to understand and explain what is happening to us. As knowledge and understanding grew, luck and superstition became less important, but the remnants are still with us today. You often hear people use luck to rationalize many of the events in their daily lives.

There's a film called *The Gods Must Be Crazy*. Although it's a comedy, the movie illustrates what superstition must have been like thousands of years ago. It's the story of a Bushman tribe in Africa who were living happily until a Coke bottle, tossed from small plane, lands unbroken near Xi, the principal character, who is out hunting. At first, the bottle is revered as a gift from the gods, but it was eventually discovered that the bottle had many uses. Because there was only one bottle to go around, it gave rise to emotions, such as envy, anger, and violence, which the tribe had never experienced before. Xi decides that the bottle was not from the gods and must be evil, because it has brought the village so much bad fortune. He embarks on a long trip to throw it off the end of the world, which for them was a very high cliff far from the village.

The words *luck* and *superstition* first appeared in the English language in the 1400s. *Fortune* is derived from Fortuna, the Roman goddess of fate, which became associated with the idea of luck. In Old English, the word *speed* referred to luck; it gave rise to the expression *Godspeed*, which is still in use today.

The ideas of luck and superstition are different, although they are intertwined. Some overlap between the two arises from loose definitions and interpretations. The unluckiness of the number thirteen is also part of the superstition that surrounds Friday the thirteenth.

With luck, fortunate and unfortunate things happen just by chance rather than action. However, there is more to luck than random chance. The idea is usually applied to outcomes for a person or group, where they are affected on a personal level. Luck can be applied to describe events that have happened in the past, or in anticipation of events to come.

"Art depends on luck and talent."
Francis Ford Coppola

Superstition is tied to luck. With it, your luck depends on your own actions or how the outside world acts on you. Superstition is the belief that a particular object, occurrence, or action can trigger good or bad luck for you. So if you do something, or don't do something, it somehow makes you lucky or unlucky. Outside forces can affect your luck the same way.

The idea of lucky and unlucky numbers is fascinating because just about everybody seems to have at least one. It is particularly strong when it comes to games of chance and generates millions and millions of dollars for casino operators and lotteries. You have to think that everybody in a casino has got to believe that they are going to be lucky—poker players excepted, because that game also involves an element of skill.

Lucky numbers for any individual vary widely, many of which are no doubt based on notable dates such as birthdays and anniversaries.

There is, however, one particular *unlucky* number that is an absolute standout because so many people share it: the number thirteen. The fear of thirteen or *triskaidekaphobia* is widespread in the Western world, although some go the other way and consider it to be lucky.

How many apartment buildings do you ever see with a thirteenth floor?

Otis Elevators, the world's largest elevator manufacturer, estimates that 85 percent of high-rise buildings don't have one. Some new buildings are even being constructed without fourteenth floors, presumably because condominium buyers recognize that the fourteenth floor is really the thirteenth.

The fear of Friday the thirteenth, or *friggatriskaidekaphobia,* takes the thirteen superstition to a whole new level. It appeared during the 1800s, though Fridays themselves had been considered as unlucky days since the 1400s. This might have been based on the fact that Jesus was crucified on a Friday. That makes Friday the thirteenth a double whammy, in Christian culture at least.

There are estimates that the lives of as many as twenty million Americans are affected by the fear of Friday the thirteenth. That's more than 5 percent of the total population, and it would be even higher if you exclude anyone under the age when this fear might first be learned. Curiously enough, there are fewer car accidents reported on Friday the thirteenth than any other thirteenth day of the week. Perhaps some of those 20 million friggatriskaidekaphobics must be deciding to stay close to home those days. There are typically two or three Friday the thirteenths in a year and interestingly, the thirteenth day of the month has fallen most frequently on Fridays over the past four hundred years.

> "Any month that starts on a Sunday will have a Friday the thirteenth. Does that make Sunday the first unlucky too?"
> *Author unknown*

Lucky numbers in Asia have a good deal to do with how they sound, like the English homonyms *their* and *there*. The number *eight* in Cantonese sounds a lot like *wealth*, while *four* sounds like *death*.

Any floor numbers that even include a four are frequently omitted (4, 14, 24, 34, and so on are out).

It gets subtle because combinations of numbers can take on altogether different meanings. The number 168 means "wealth for entire life" while 888 means "lots of wealth." In Mandarin, the number five sounds like "never" or "not." Fifty-four wouldn't be unlucky, in spite of the four, because it sounds like "no death."

In some countries, lucky numbers that appear in phone numbers and license plates are routinely bought and sold for large sums of money. In Asia, the rights to a phone number with all eights sold recently for more than a quarter of a million dollars. That particular phone number must be priceless to a telemarketing firm—who wouldn't pick up the call? And besides, it might be bad luck not to. What do you think you could get for a telephone number with all fours?

Surely, ideas like luck, lucky numbers, numerology, astrology, tarot cards, and the like should all be seen in the same way that many view lottery tickets and gambling games that don't involve strategy, tactics, or even the slightest element of skill. They really should be just for fun and games.

Sigmund Freud and many other psychologists believe that the idea of luck has a lot to do with one's own thinking and actually can become self-fulfilling. Many people who believe in luck and consider themselves to be lucky are often happier and more successful individuals. If you could learn to think this way, do you think it would become self-reinforcing and possibly work for you?

> "In the long run, you make your own luck—good, bad or indifferent."
> *Loretta Lynn*

Luck is all well and good, but it comes in handier when you combine it with hard work. Here are three quotes to illustrate the point:

"The best luck of all is the luck you make for yourself."
—*General Douglas MacArthur*

"No one has as much luck around the greens
as the one who practices a lot."
—*Chi Chi Rodriguez*

"Luck is a dividend of sweat. The more
you sweat, the luckier you get."
—*Ray Kroc*

There is a peculiar kind of luck called *serendipity*. It's really more of a happy accident and is seen as a windfall. It happens in situations where you find one thing when you were looking for something else. I bet that some of the greatest works of modern art started with an accidental drop of paint. Christopher Columbus discovered America by accident simply because he was looking for a shortcut to East India. Serendipity even led to the discovery of penicillin in 1928. Alexander Fleming accidentally left a bacteria sample open; a mold got onto it that killed the bacteria. From this stroke of luck, Fleming went on to discover his lifesaving antibiotic, penicillin. Many other notable inventions that came about by serendipity include: chocolate chip cookies, inkjet printers, Post-it notes, Velcro, saccharin, potato chips, and even Coca-Cola.

"Name the greatest of all inventors. Accident."
Mark Twain

There's a great quote from the film *Dirty Harry*:

"I know what you're thinking. Did he fire six shots or
only five? Well, to tell you the truth, in all this excitement
I kind of lost track myself. But being as this is a .44
Magnum, the most powerful handgun in the world, and
would blow your head clean off, you've got to ask yourself
one question: Do I feel lucky? Well, do ya, punk?"

Now that's one good question about luck.

In addition to the fear of the number thirteen, people are superstitious about things like black cats crossing their paths, walking under ladders (maybe that's just common sense), and breaking mirrors. And there are many more, both good and bad. If they ever appear to work out, even if only a couple of times, it surely greatly strengthens people's own superstitions.

There are lots of different groups of people, each with their own set superstitions that have developed over the years.

Sailors, for instance, have always had lots of superstitions. Imagine sailing in the middle of an ocean 200 years ago during a raging storm in what amounted to nothing more than a tiny little wooden world that was very much at the mercy of nature. No wonder those sailors believed in luck and superstition. Who wouldn't?

> "Touch wood. Scratch a stay. Turn around three times. May the Lord and saints preserve us."
> *Master and Commander*

Actors believe that it's bad luck to say "good luck" before a play. That's where the expression "break a leg" comes from. Some actors also believe that Shakespeare's *Macbeth* is cursed. They only refer to it in theatres as the "Scottish Play."

If you want to talk about a really superstitious group of people, take a look at the world of sports. There are loads of superstitions in just about every game.

Baseball is filled with a rich history of superstition, including the Curse of the Bambino, where the Red Socks went without winning a World Series for decades after they traded Babe Ruth to the New York Yankees. It all makes America's game even more entertaining and interesting.

> "I had only one superstition. I made sure to touch all the bases when I hit a home run."
> Babe Ruth, *the Bambino*

Have you ever noticed all the rituals that baseball players go through before they even think about swinging a bat? Step into the batters box. Touch the plate. Take a practice swing. Step out. Touch your helmet. Rub your elbow and then tap each shoe. Is it the left one first? Only then are they ready to stand up to the plate and take a swing. And they'll probably even want to the touch the plate one more time before taking their stance.

Many point out, however, that these routines are not rituals for luck. They're meant to help focus players' minds on the task at hand.

Professional golfers are a pretty similar bunch. As in baseball, they also carefully follow pre-shot routines, which are regarded as part of getting their heads into the right place before hitting a shot or a putt. Put them out of their routine—say a fly lands on the ball—and they step away from it and start the whole routine all over again. I don't think there's anyone who wouldn't call that a ritual.

"The secret of achievement is to hold a picture of a successful outcome in the mind."
Henry David Thoreau

Tiger Woods always wears a red shirt and black pants in Sunday's final round. He claims that it's because his mother says that they are his *power colors*. If you took them away from him, however, he might not have performed anywhere nearly as well as he has. Why does he wear the same uniform only on Sunday afternoons? Superstition aside, there might be a psychological element to it because it announces to the field, "It's Sunday, and I'm here to *win*." And the more he won with that red shirt on, the greater the impact it probably had on the minds of the other players. Then again, red is also the color of Stanford University, his alma mater.

There are plenty of highly educated and otherwise skeptical people with lucky charms like rabbits' feet, four-leaf clovers, or charm bracelets. The idea of these kinds of amulets must go back to the most ancient of times, particularly when they might have been believed to ward off evil. Many thousands of years ago, there must have been many tribes living in the wilderness that needed comfort. It's possible that amulets had become such a big part of their culture, and the ideas became so ingrained that they have been passed on to us today. Have you ever wondered why upset

"If you think you can, you can. And if you think you can't, you're right."
Mary Kay Ash, Cosmetics

children cling to teddy bears? On the surface, it's probably best explained as seeking comfort from something that represents their mother. Like the teddy bear, amulets provide comfort and maybe somehow work in a similar way. Besides, who would want to walk down Wall Street with a teddy bear in his briefcase?

There are as many examples of unlucky objects. The Hope Diamond (*Le bleu de France*) and Ancient Egyptian artifacts looted from tombs are believed to curse their owners. Cursed objects are featured in popular films such as *Indiana Jones* and *Pirates of the Caribbean.*

What if you accidentally do something that you believe will bring on bad luck? Is there any way to undo it? The answer is yes, and the belief in it is like preventive medicine. That's the idea, at least.

United States two-dollar bills are largely uncirculated because they are generally believed to be unlucky, but if you ever get one, you can undo the bad luck by folding a corner over. If you were to receive one with four corners already folded over, you might be best off to pass on it.

> "Sure, luck means a lot in football. Not having a good quarterback is bad luck."
> Don Shula

I also understand that it is practically illegal for elderly aunts to not throw salt over their shoulder after spilling some. I think it's supposed to be the left one. I wonder if it would better if you covered both? Or would that make it worse?

What about the Titanic? Unsinkable? Maybe the White Star Line shouldn't have said that out loud because it was seen as a *jinx* when she sank on her maiden voyage, killing 1,517 people. If only the owners of the Titanic had knocked on wood after calling her unsinkable, it might have worked out differently. That's the idea, at least.

> "I busted a mirror and got seven years bad luck. My lawyer thinks he can get me five."
> *Steven Wright*

Experimental psychologist B. F. Skinner, from the previous chapter, turned understanding superstition into a science. Armed again solely with pigeons, seeds, and a dispensing machine, he observed bizarre individual rituals develop among the birds in attempts to get more food. He interpreted these as a form of superstition. Some spun around in circles, while others waved their heads, their feet, and displayed all kinds of unusual behavior. When they eventually got a seed after repeated rituals, it reinforced their behavior. Skinner believed that the pigeons thought that their behavior was connected with their feeding. After enough rewards, they would never give them up. Some even performed their rituals thousands of times to get a single seed.

In the end, even if you think it's silly, there appears to be no shortage of reasons why someone might believe in luck.

Web Search Keywords

| *frank sinatra luck* | *gods must be crazy trailer* | *dirty harry do you feel lucky* | *curse of the bambino* | *hope diamond* | *titanic trailer* | *bf skinner video* |

Chapter 17

Stay or Switch?

The TV game show *Let's Make a Deal,* hosted by Monty Hall, was around for ages. Its heyday was from 1963 to 1976, but it subsequently reappeared with different hosts for numerous other seasons and in a number of other countries. It consisted of a handful of games where contestants, called *traders*, chose between different boxes and other things to win unrevealed prizes. During the show, they'd trade off what they'd already won in an attempt to win even bigger prizes.

> "Actually, I'm an overnight success, but it took twenty years."
> *Monty Hall, Let's Make A Deal*

In the last round, the finalist would choose between one of three doors to win the grand prize. Behind one of the doors was a really big prize, perhaps a car or a boat. The other two hid bad prizes, called *zonks,* like toasters, blenders, and sometimes even live animals like goats.

Which particular door chosen doesn't really matter, because each door has an equal one-in-three chance of winning. Let's say it was door number one. Monty Hall knows what's behind all three doors and opens up one of the two remaining doors. He opens door number three and reveals a toaster. He's always going to show you a zonk; otherwise it wouldn't be much of a game. So now we know that there's a car behind one of the two remaining doors.

Monty Hall then asks a seemingly simple question that's become known as the *Monty Hall problem*. He asks you if you want to stay with your original pick or switch to the other unopened door.

What should you do?

Questions like this come up in game theory all the time. Many, or maybe most people might say that it doesn't matter because with only two doors left to open, they have an equal chance of hiding a car. Some might even say, "Besides, I'm feeling lucky today, so I'll stay with door number one." Oddly enough, it doesn't quite work that way.

A notable article appeared in *Parade* magazine (1990) in a column called "Ask Marilyn." Its author Marilyn vos Savant rose to fame in 1986 when the *Guinness Book of World Records* listed her as having the highest IQ (228). Some argued at the time that chess player Bobby Fisher's IQ was probably much higher.

Her answer to the question was to *always* switch and it created something of a fuss. The magazine received more than ten thousand letters, including at least one thousand from academics, many with PhDs, who completely disagreed with her. Psychologist Massimo Piattelli-Palmarini said, "No other puzzle comes so close to fooling all of the people all of the time," after a group study revealed that only 10 percent of the participants chose to switch.

When you picked door number one, you had a one-in-three chance of winning, and Monty inherited a two-in-three chance. Strange as it seems to some, after Monty revealed a zonk, his remaining unopened door still had a two-in-three chance. He had a two-in-three chance of winning before, so why would that change to 50-50 (one-in-two) after he opens a door? If you stay with door number one, you're still stuck at one-in-three. If you switch, you double your chances of winning.

> "I'd rather fight than switch"
> *1960s tobacco advertisement*

If you aren't convinced, the table below illustrates another way to get you to the answer. There are only three ways to mix one car and two blenders behind the three doors. (I think there's a joke in there somewhere.)

Door 1	Door 2	Door 3	Stay	Switch
Car	Blender	Blender	Car	Blender
Blender	Car	Blender	Blender	Car
Blender	Blender	Car	Blender	Car

If you stay (illustrated in the fourth column), you should expect to end up with one car and two blenders over time. But if you were to switch (the fifth column), you'd expect to win two cars, which is twice as good.

There is another way to think about it if you're still not convinced. Call it a game about game theory. In a follow up article, Marilyn encouraged teachers of grade schools to have their classrooms try the game, and it was a hit with the students.

You need to play it with a friend. You'll need three playing cards, like an ace and two 2s. It's even better to use index cards where you write answers on the card like: car, blender, toaster; or Super Bowl ring, malaria, smallpox. One of you is going to take on the role of Monty Hall.

> "Thanks for that fun math problem. I really enjoyed it. It got me out of fractions for two days! Got any more?"
> *Middle school student*

Shuffle the three cards and lay them out face down. The contestant selects a card, but isn't allowed to look. Monty Hall gets to look at the other two, but without you seeing them. Monty turns over one of the two unselected cards, which should always be a bad one. Now you, as the contestant, must decide whether to stay or switch.

Try it ten times in a row, maybe once where you always stay and then another ten times where you switch. Keep track of your winnings and see what happens. If it doesn't work out the first time, try counting twenty rounds in case you need more turns for the averages to work out.

There's a good lesson that you can take away from this problem that might help sometime if you face a similar dilemma. Think of extremes.

Zeno is thought to have introduced the method of proof called *reductio ad absurdum*, meaning "reduction to the absurd." Instead of three doors, let's say that the game incorporated a million doors. You pick one, say door 132,768. Monty then reveals all 999,998 remaining doors except yours and his. How do you feel about his chances of winning the car?

There's a related puzzle that's been around even longer. Let's say that you've been in touch with a dog breeder who has two puppies. You want a male dog but would take both if they're both are males. The breeder tells you that at least one of them is male. What are the odds that the other one is male too?

Just about everybody I've ever asked has said that it's 50-50, but it's actually only one in three. It's easy to spot when you write down the only combinations of male and female dogs: MM, MF, FM, and FF. There are three combinations that have at least one male, but only one of the three has two males.

Sometimes seemingly new questions have already been asked and answered years before. Monty Hall and the dog breeder problems are both variations on a paradox proposed in 1889, called *Bertrand's box*. In it you are presented with three boxes: one with two gold coins, one with two silver coins, and one with one of each. You pick a box and pull out a coin. If it's gold, what is the chance that the other remaining coin in the box is gold as well? Like before, many people might think that there's a 50-50 chance. But again, it doesn't work that way. It turns out to be a chance of two in three. Think about the six coins in the three boxes individually and how many ways there are to get gold-gold versus gold-silver after you eliminate silver-gold and silver-silver.

Questions, even if they're only on a game show, always make you think, and sometimes the answers are subtler than you might expect.

Web Search Keywords

| *monty hall simulator* | *game theory* | *movie 21 explains the monty hall problem*| *monty hall* | *let's make a deal* | *bertrands box* |

Chapter 18

The Art of Selling Valuable Baseball Cards

There's a curious problem that has provoked a fair bit of thought over the years. This version puts it into a contemporary context.

The most rare and valuable baseball card right now is probably the Honus Wagner T206 card. It was issued from 1909 to 1911. Wagner played for the Pittsburgh Pirates from 1897 to 1917 and was the greatest player of his time. That begs the question: "What happened to the 1912 to 1917 cards?" Well, Honus wasn't in favor of smoking, let alone endorsing tobacco sales. When the 1909 to 1911 cards started being included in cigarette packages, he butted them out, so to speak.

> "I knew my career was over. In 1965 my baseball card came out with no picture."
> *Bob Uecker, Mr. Baseball*

A near mint-condition T206 card sold in 2007 for $2.8 million, the highest price ever for a baseball card. Interestingly, hockey legend Wayne Gretzky once owned that particular card. He, along with several partners, purchased it for $500,000 in 1992.

Let's say that you and someone else, someone you don't know, each own identical baseball cards from a long time ago. They're the only two remaining cards in the world, and both are in mint condition, making them very valuable.

An astute and wealthy collector figures that if he owned both, they'd be worth even more to him. Sometimes in economics, one plus one can actually equal more than two (although at other times, it could be less). He plans to contact each of you separately, buy both cards, and then tear one of them in half. That would leave him with the only remaining card, which he figures would be worth even more than the value of the two combined. If you're ever thinking about trying anything like this for yourself, you might want to test the market before you do any ripping. But I'll leave that up to you.

> "Two plus two equals fish."
> *George Orwell, 1984*

His proposal is simple.

He's prepared to pay you up to $10 million each for your cards, but only if you both agree to sell them at the same time. He asks you to tell him your price, but neither card owner knows what the other asks. If you knew that the previously most valuable card had just sold for around $3 million, the buyer's offer would have to sound pretty intriguing.

To make the sale more competitive, and so the collector can extract the lowest possible purchase price for the cards, he adds a few wrinkles. He says that he will pay each of you the lesser of your two prices. The lower bidder will get a $2 million bonus, but the higher bidder will suffer a $2 million penalty. In a tie, you'd both get the same price. In any cooperative arrangement, you'd obviously try to contact each other and agree to go in at $10 million apiece. However, the world doesn't always work that way. And remember, you have no way of getting in touch.

So, what's your price?

Ten million dollars seems like a pretty good starting point for each of you, but then again, maybe not. If I was smart and thought that you might be inclined to cooperate by bidding $10 million, then I should bid nine. That would set the price at nine. I'd get eleven million (nine plus two from the bonus) and you'd get seven (nine minus the two from the penalty). But if I were smarter still, I'd realize that you're almost certainly thinking about exactly the same strategy, so there's no way you're ever going to bid ten, and probably not even nine, maybe eight? But then I would figure that you'd be thinking exactly the same thing about me.

This uncooperative thinking carries on for a while and drives our tentative prices successively lower. At first blush, some might think that it could actually get us all the way down to zero. For example, if I was to bid one, you could bid zero and end up with two. So I might as well bid zero too, but that's not good for either of us because we'd both end up with nothing. Instead, we should both conclude that if we set our prices at two, we would get $2 million each, and it would work out best for both of us. It all hinges on the penalty and bonus.

> "That's weird, wild stuff"
> *Johnny Carson*

This might strike you as rather odd. At least I hope it does, because then it made you think.

The best solutions to games like this are based on something called the *Nash equilibrium*. It's an important concept in everything from economics and how companies set competitive pricing, to military strategy, traffic flow, auctions, genetic evolution, and even steroid use in the Olympics. John Nash struggled with severe mental health issues throughout most of his life. Despite that, he eventually went on to win the Nobel Prize in Economics for his work. There's a movie called *A Beautiful Mind* based on his life that's well worth watching.

Web Search Keywords
| *valuable baseball cards* | *honus wagner* | *john nash* | *a beautiful mind* | *nash equilibrium youtube* |

Chapter 19

Friend or Foe?

There's another curious problem related to the baseball card game from the previous chapter known as the *prisoner's dilemma.* This version is called *he said—she said.*

Let's say that you, or your twin sister, accidentally break a valuable vase one night when your parents are out. Next morning, there's big trouble and your mother demands to know who is responsible.

She talks to each of you *separately* and offers up the same bargain. Her deal has four conditions:

- If you rat on your twin, and she keeps her mouth shut, you get off free and clear; and your sibling loses her allowance for a whole year.
- If you keep quiet, and she rats on you, then you lose your allowance for a whole year, while she walks away.
- If you both rat, you both lose your allowances for three months.
- If you both keep your mouths shut, you both lose your allowances for only one month.

"Parents are not interested in justice, they're interested in peace and quiet."
Bill Cosby

The last case suggests that your mother is willing to be lenient because she recognizes that you're trying to look out for each other. Something tells me that most mothers might not exactly offer up that bargain, but hey, this is just a game.

Aside from the morality of lying, the real question is this: "Should you blame the other or remain silent?"

The best strategy turns out to be *always rat*. That might come as a surprise because both of you would do better by cooperating and both keeping your mouths shut. I think this should be called "the Bart Simpson response," because he probably would have come up with the answer intuitively.

Think of it this way. From your perspective, your sister can either keep quiet or rat. Let's start with she shuts up. If you keep quiet as well, you'll both lose your allowances for one month, but if you rat you'll walk away without a penalty. So if she keeps quiet, you should rat. If your sister instead chooses to rat, and you keep quiet, you'll lose your allowance for an entire year. If you rat, you'll both lose your allowances for three months. So if she rats, you should rat too. Even though you would do better collectively by both keeping your mouths shut, from each of your perspectives both of you always fare better by ratting. This is another example of the Nash equilibrium from the previous chapter.

There have been game shows based on this problem, including *Friend or Foe?* It aired in 2002 and ran on American television for several seasons. There have also been some UK and Australian series as well. There was even a Manga TV series based on the problem that aired in Japan.

The themes for the shows were all pretty similar. A number of contestants would compete by answering questions with winnings contributing to a pool of cash. When it got down to the final two players, they had to decide to cooperate (friend) or not to (foe). If they cooperated, they would split the pool. If there was one friend and one foe, then the foe took everything. If there were two foes, they both walk away with nothing.

There's an interesting game that lets you explore this seemingly odd idea even further. If you were to face the he said—she said game

"Play it again, Sam"
Casablanca, misquoted

just once, you've already seen why you should always rat out each other. What if you were to play the game repeatedly? Could you learn to cooperate occasionally and find a strategy that lets you both do better over time?

Let's say that you and your sister are on a game show, and each of you has two buttons. One button is to keep quiet (cooperate) and displays a happy face. The other is to rat (not cooperate, sometimes called defect) and displays an angry face.

The game is played in rounds. Each of you presses one of your buttons and the faces are revealed at the same time.

- If there's one happy face and one angry face, the angry face gets 500 points, and the happy face gets zero.
- If there are two angry faces, both get 100 points.
- With two happy faces, it's 300 points each.

You play the game for a while. The twin with the higher number of points at the end of the game is declared the winner. The point about playing it for a *while* is subtle. It's taken from an idea that came up in the previous chapter. If we play a fixed number of rounds, say a ten-round game, the final round is really just a single round version of the game from before. We already know that the best outcome for both of you is to rat, by pressing angry face buttons. Wouldn't that make the ninth round really just another last round as well? That would also call for two angry faces. Like the baseball card game, this kind of thinking keeps backtracking and would eventually result in angry faces from the start. So for a legitimate game, neither of you can know in advance how many rounds it will involve. The easiest way to do this is for the game show host to end the game without warning.

If you both play angry faces, neither of you will ever get ahead. If you both always cooperate, you'll always end in a tie as well. The game might work better if the host adds an extra rule that neither of you is awarded a prize in the event of a tie, or even for a close score. This would encourage you to mix up your play in an attempt to gain an edge.

This game is known as the *repeated* or *iterated* prisoner's dilemma. It's very popular with people who study game theory, as well as computer programmers who like to write programs to fight it out over many rounds. There are tournaments that are based on the game. They're meant to help understand it better and try to identify if any superior strategies might exist. Besides, it's always fun to compete.

It turns out that there is one very simple approach that is tough to beat, called *tit for tat*. It starts by playing nice, and opens with a happy face. Its following moves are based entirely on how the other player responded in each previous round. If an angry face was played against your initial happy face, you would retaliate in the next round by playing an angry face, and so on.

Some programs incorporate variations to this strategy by occasionally playing an unexpected angry face for no particular reason other than to stir things up. That sounds a bit like some people I know.

This deceptively simple game has extraordinary implications in natural science, including animal behavior and evolution. It turns out that there are a lot of prisoner's dilemma games going on in nature, and in our lives, all the time. And they've been going on for a very long time.

If you want to learn more, I recommend *The Selfish Gene*, by Richard Dawkins, an international bestseller first published in 1976. You should start with chapter 12, titled "Nice Guys Finish First," but it all makes for fascinating reading.

Web Search Keywords

| *prisoners dilemma game* | *repeated prisoners dilemma strategies* | *dilbert prisoners dilemma* | *friend or foe premier* | *tit for tat* | *selfish gene youtube* |

Chapter 20

Why Do Things Move the Way They Do?

"Newton got beaned by the apple good,
Yeah, yeah, yeah, yeah"
—REM, Man on the Moon

Sir Isaac Newton changed the world more than three hundred years ago. He could have achieved more only if he'd also invented the Fig Newton, which is "a tasty snack that can be enjoyed throughout your day," at least according to Christie Brothers.

Newton figured out how to describe all the motion that we see going on in the world around us, including the motions of the earth, the moon, and the planets. It was a truly remarkable feat. He achieved all this by discovering three fundamental laws of motion as well as the law of universal gravitation. As the story goes, he originally got the idea for gravity and how the earth pulls everything toward it when an apple fell from a tree and hit a sleeping Newton on the head. All of his discoveries must have come from asking himself: "Why do things move in the way they do?" He wrote all about it in 1678 in his work *Principia* (*Philosophiae Naturalis Principia*

Mathematica, which is Latin for *Mathematical Principles of Natural Philosophy*).

Newton's Three Laws of Motion
1. The First Law

> *Every body continues in its state of rest, or of uniform motion in a right line, unless it is compelled to change that state by forces impressed upon it.*

The first law, sometimes referred to as the *law of inertia*, is usually written in modern textbooks as something like: "A body at rest tends to remain at rest, while a body in motion tends to remain in motion, unless acted upon by an external force." That might translate into contemporary language as something more like: "Apples on your table don't start moving around by themselves, and if you launch one from your balcony, it's going to keep on falling until it hits the pavement."

One good way to see the first law in action is by fooling around with the puck on an air-hockey table or rolling balls on a billiards table. Billiard balls provide great illustrations for all three laws.

While the apple might have prompted Newton to think about gravity, the idea that moving bodies don't change course unless something forces them may well have solidified his thinking. He must have realized that the moon orbits the earth because the earth is somehow pulling on it, just like the apple.

2. The Second Law

> *The change of motion is proportional to the motive force impressed; and is made in the direction of the right line in which that force is impressed.*

That means the harder you push something, the faster it accelerates, and always in the direction you push it. At the risk of including an equation here, the second law is usually written out as Newton's famous equation $F=ma$, where F is force applied to an

> "All you need to know to pass first year physics is $F=ma$. But you have to know it well."
> *Physics Professor*

object, m is its mass, and a is the resulting acceleration. You can use it, along with gravity and some of his mathematics, to calculate almost everything about motion you see going on all around you. If I were to drop an apple from my twentieth-floor balcony, it would be easy to calculate how long it would take it to hit the pavement. I'm not suggesting that you go out and try this, because you might accidentally hit somebody on the head, and twenty stories is a lot higher up than Newton's apple tree. Mankind's understanding of Newton's second law and gravity made it possible for us to get to the moon and back.

If you want to see the second law in action for yourself, take a soccer ball and give it a little kick. Then kick it harder. It always goes where you're kicking it, and the harder you kick it, the farther it will go. It works well with billiard balls too.

3. The Third Law

To every action there is always opposed an equal reaction; or, mutual actions of two bodies upon each other are always equal, and directed to contrary parts.

Most modern textbooks include only the first bit: "To every action there is an equal and opposite reaction."

You will most definitely feel the full effect of the third law if punch a brick wall as hard as you can. That's because the wall punches back. And if you actually were to try this, it would make you an idiot.

> "For every action, there is an equal and opposite criticism."
> *Steven Wright*

There's a fun experiment you can try. It works best if you already know how to skate and it's not minus forty degrees outside. Stand face-to-face with a friend, both of you on skates, then one of you push the other. You might think that if I push my friend, she'll go backwards and I'll stay put. But we actually both go backwards. That's because when I push her, she's also pushing me back.

To see this with billiard balls is subtle, but it works exactly the same way. When I hit the cue ball at another ball, provided that I hit it straight on, the ball I hit carries on at the same speed and direction that the cue ball was moving. According to Newton's third law, the ball I hit pushes the cue ball back with an equal and opposite force and stops it. If not for that, *both* balls would keep rolling.

It's slightly more complicated if the balls don't collide exactly head on, but the result is based on the same idea, although it takes a bit of arithmetic to explain.

That's Newton's third law in action, and that's all there is to it: If I push something, it pushes me back.

I came across something funny about Newton's three laws based on an old joke that just about everybody has heard:

Q: Why did the chicken cross the road?
A: To get to the other side.

To rephrase Newton's laws in chicken language, they might go something like this:

1. Chickens at rest on the sidewalk tend to remain on the sidewalk, while chickens in motion tend to cross the road.
2. Any chicken that crosses the road might very well have been pushed.
3. If one chicken pushes another one across the road, it would in turn be pushed away from the road.

> "Yesterday I saw a chicken crossing the road. I asked it why. It told me it was none of my business."
> *Steven Wright*

Newton's ideas upset two thousand years of thinking. The Ancient Greeks, most notably Aristotle, believed that force was necessary just to maintain steady motion. Aristotle said: "No motion without force." It's hardly surprising, because when they looked at a cart, it stopped moving if the ox stopped pulling. Newton's world was an idealized one, without friction or air resistance.

Another great part about Newton's story is that Sir Isaac invented an advanced form of mathematics called *calculus* that he needed to complete his calculations of motion, which in itself was an absolutely amazing feat. He laid out most of the foundations of his greatest works in his twenties. While he was at it, he also invented and built the first refracting telescope, which is the design of all large telescopes today including the Hubble space telescope.

"Many people die at twenty-five and aren't buried until they're seventy-five."
Benjamin Franklin

So, if you're not twenty yet, or even if you're pushing ninety, it's time to get busy!

Web Search Keywords

| *newton's laws lego* | *gravity* | *newton's three laws* | *calculus* | *scariest roller-coasters* | *rem man on the moon video* | *big fig newton commercial*|

Chapter 21

Wile E. Coyote—Supergenius, or What?

"Road Runner, the Coyote's after you.
Road Runner, if he catches you, you're through."
—*Warner Brothers*

When I was studying science in college, some friends and I used to get a kick out of watching cartoons and competing to see who could count the most physical laws being broken. I know it sounds like something from the TV series *The Big Bang Theory*, but it seemed like a good way to put off working on homework assignments at the time.

> I like nonsense, it wakes up the brain cells."
> *Dr. Seuss*

One of the best shows for our game was *Road Runner* on Saturday mornings. It pits the Coyote against the Road Runner. The basic plot for every episode was for the Coyote to try to catch the Road Runner with one of his zany contraptions or schemes. They never quite worked out, although the cartoonists at least always gave him a fighting chance.

For a self-proclaimed "supergenius," Wile E. sure had some wacky ideas about the way nature works.

One of my all-time favorites was from the episode "Ready … Set … Zoom." In it, he stood on roller skates and strapped an Acme outboard motor onto his backside. Then he put it into a washtub that was on top of a Jim Dandy wagon. His idea was to speed across the desert and catch the Road Runner. It seemed to be going well until he saw "Danger Bridge Out." You can easily figure out, armed with even just a bit of Newton's science, that this has absolutely no chance of working in the real world. All the pushing and pulling would cancel each other and the motor would only stir up the water in the barrel. But it was always great fun to watch.

The Coyote also invented a similar contraption involving a skateboard with a sail and an electric fan. It likewise seemed to get off to a good start, although he didn't fare very well in the end, as usual.

The popular television series *Mythbusters* touches on this in an episode that "busts" a video showing a great mass of bees glued to a laptop computer that manage to lift it into the air. As it turned out, it flew with a little help from some fishing microfilament.

The Coyote's supplies were always delivered by Acme Corporation, a mail order company. I was once watching Road Runner with my kids, who were quite young at the time. They asked, "If he could buy all this stuff from Acme, why doesn't he just buy food?" Good question. I explained to them that sometimes you have to ignore reality and accept odd situations for fun.

Among my other favorite natural law-breakings in Coyote science was that gravity never quite applied to him, at least in any conventional sense. He truly was an exception to Newton's laws. I lost track of how many times he'd fly off a cliff and remain suspended in mid-air for two or three seconds, until he looked down. Then he always ended up at the bottom of a canyon. Maybe it inspired the phrase "Just don't look down."

> "I know this defies the law of gravity, but you see, I never studied law."
> *Bugs Bunny*

Dehydrated boulders and earthquake pills also gave him trouble. Apparently, they're not effective on roadrunners anyway. That's why it's always a good idea to read the label. He missed where it read, "Not effective on roadrunners."

I'll always remember an episode where the Coyote caught a fly out of the air with his hand and ate it. It prompted me to give it try one day and I learned that it most certainly could be done, but the fly didn't taste all that great. But yet again, some of the laws of Coyote science are a bit dodgy. He played it like an overhand tennis serve. But if you try to grab a fly with an open palm, or even hit it with newspaper, a cushion of air will push the fly away. The trick is to go at it sideways, like a karate chop, with your hand in the shape of a cup, and then encircle the little devil.

Now for the best Road Runner question of all time: "Is it *beep beep*, or *meep meep*?" It always sounded a bit like both to me. Guess it depends on your mood.

Web Search Keywords

| *road runner* | *wile e coyote gravity lessons* | *wile e coyote science* | *wile e coyote outboard motor* | *wile e coyote bugs bunny video* |

Chapter 22

Can Anybody Turn Lead into Gold?

That's got to be the best $64,000 question of all time: "Is it really possible to turn lead into gold?"

Isaac Newton thought he could. Besides, who wouldn't want to try? When I think about Newton and how he profoundly changed everything by describing the world so precisely with carefully written laws, equations, and mathematics, it strikes me as rather surprising that he decided to go off on this tangent.

> "Remember the golden rule. What's that? Whoever has the gold makes the rules."
> *The Wizard of Id*

He and other scientists at the time, known as *alchemists*, believed that it was possible to turn one element into another. It was a pretty popular idea back then, called *transmutation* of the elements. Although he lived into his eighties, Newton died from a form of poisoning that came from playing around with too many chemicals. Heavy metals like lead, mercury, and others that he worked with are pretty toxic and better left alone, or at least ought to be handled very carefully. Many believe that the elevated levels of lead and other toxins in his system eventually gave rise to some peculiar behavior that appeared in his later life.

Alchemy dates back thousands of years and eventually gave rise to many modern sciences, including chemistry, metallurgy, and medicine. It tried to combine describing how the world works with mythology, religion, and even wizardry.

One of the early objectives of alchemy was to find the *philosopher's stone,* which was believed to possess the power to turn base metals into gold. It had the added benefit of being an elixir of life that would heal any ailment and, therefore, grant immortality. *Magnum opus* (Latin for "big work") was the term used to describe any attempt to find the stone. The idea even appears in *Harry Potter and the Philosopher's Stone*. In the story, the only existing stone is hidden somewhere at Hogwarts and guarded by a giant three-headed dog. These kinds of tales all give us a great sense of what alchemy must have been like in its heyday.

> Voldemort to Harry: "But there is something that can [give me a body of my own]; something that, conveniently enough, lies in your pocket."
> *Harry Potter*

Much of alchemy came from seventh- and eighth-century Islam. Its name is derived from the word *al-kimia*. Jabir ibn Hayyan (722–804 AD) introduced discipline to it with methods and experiments that gave the field more of what we would consider as science today. Some consider him to be the father of modern chemistry, though many would argue that Robert Boyle (1627–1691) deserves the credit. He made a real science of it.

Jabir and others contributed greatly to chemistry with the discovery of various acids, including muriatic acid (more commonly known as hydrochloric acid), sulfuric acid, and nitric acid. Their *aqua regia*, a mixture of nitric and hydrochloric acids, was capable of dissolving gold; it served to strengthen their belief in the possibility of making gold.

Jabir also invented the elemental system that was adopted in medieval alchemy. His original system consisted of seven elements, including the five classical elements from ancient times (ether, air, earth, fire, and water), plus two new ones representing the metals: sulfur (combustibility or fire) and mercury (metallic properties). This

> "He has the Midas touch. Everything he touches turns into a Muffler."
> *Henny Youngman*

system eventually grew into eight elements by adding in a dash of salt, which he believed was responsible for making things solid. His study of materials gave rise to early versions of the periodic table, which today is one of the cornerstones of modern chemistry. Alchemy lives on in the *New Age* movement that developed in the middle of the twentieth century.

Turning lead into gold is one thing, and would be a very good thing at that, but the alchemists also imagined they could create life in a laboratory—even human life. We're still playing that game, at least the last time I checked.

Stanley Miller and Harold Urey carried out an experiment at the University of Chicago in 1952 that simulated the conditions believed to have existed on earth billions of years ago. It included a reaction vessel partly filled with water, meant to simulate the oceans. Also in the vessel were carbon dioxide, nitrogen, hydrogen sulfide, and sulfur dioxide, all thought to have been present in earth's early atmosphere. After passing an electrical discharge through these gases for several weeks, something strange began to happen when the water began to take on the color of tea. In the brew, they found amino acids, the building blocks of DNA—the basis of life. This was the first scientific experiment that attempted to explain the origin of life, and it may well have been inspired by a simple question like: "What if?"

Alchemy and the idea of transmutation fell out of favor in the eighteenth century, when modern chemistry became accepted as legitimate science. The story picks up again with the advent of nuclear science.

In 1901, Ernst Rutherford and Frederick Soddy discovered that transmutation really does exist in nature. Thorium atoms sometimes turn into radium through the process of *radioactive decay*. You'll read more about it in chapter 25. Rutherford later went on to discover an artificial way to convert nitrogen into oxygen atoms by bombarding them with subatomic particles. Rutherford was sensitive to the term transmutation because he was afraid he might be labeled an alchemist. Nevertheless, he was certainly onto something big.

Following Rutherford's discoveries, transmutation became a curiosity once again. It became the basis of many experiments carried out in nuclear physics-related laboratories and facilities such as power plants and particle accelerators. Scientists eventually managed to perform the amazing feat of turning lead into gold. But the alchemists were doomed to failure anyway because turning lead into gold costs much more in energy than the gold is worth. To make matters worse, the manufactured gold was unstable and typically lasted less than a minute. But at least it was a nice try.

If it's so hard to make, where did all the gold come from in the first place? Moreover, where does any of what makes up the world actually come from including carbon, which is the stuff of life? Many might think that metals like iron, silver, and gold just come from some hole in the ground and have been there forever. But that is not their entire history.

It turns out that the cosmos is really one giant alchemist. Everything in our world, from carbon on up, including elements like silver and gold, is not from our world, but came out of exploding stars through a process called *nucleosynthesis*. And when you think about it that way, doesn't it make gold seem even more precious?

"We are stardust. We are golden. And we've got to get ourselves back to the garden."
Joni Mitchell

"There's gold in them thar hills!" Or maybe that should be "them thar oceans!" There really is gold dissolved in the oceans, even though it's in exceedingly small concentrations, being only about six parts per trillion. On the other hand, water covers 70 percent of the earth's surface, so that adds up to a lot of gold. The volume of the world's oceans is estimated to be slightly more than one billion cubic kilometers, which could hold roughly 300 million ounces of gold, or fifty times all the gold ever produced by mankind. Yet again, however, it costs more to extract than the gold is worth.

There are other interesting ways that you can turn metal into gold. Have you ever wondered how much pennies, nickels, or dimes are really worth? It's pretty easy to figure out. All you need to know is the mass of the coin, its composition, and the current prices of the metals it's made from. When metal prices are high, people have actually been known to melt down coins and sell the metal for more than face value. You can look up melt values of coins every day at www.coinflation.com.

I was talking to a friend of mine a while back who raised an interesting question: "Isn't it illegal to destroy currency?"

I didn't know for sure, but it turns out that in the United States it is only illegal to *deface* coins, particularly when it comes to alterations in order to make them look like miss minted collectors items, which would be considered fraud. People have been melting coins for decades. But check with a lawyer first if you plan on melting four oil barrels worth of pennies, nickels, dimes, or whatever. Burning or otherwise destroying banknotes (or bills) is technically illegal, but who would ever even dream of burning a sack of twenties?

"It costs a fortune to heat this place." *Cliffhanger – as Gabe burns money to keep warm inside a cave.*

One neat thing about trying to do this with pennies is that they come in two forms. US pennies dated from 1909 to 1982 weigh 3.1 or 3.2 grams, while those minted after 1982 weigh only 2.5 grams. The older pennies are 95 percent copper and are currently worth significantly more than one cent (in early 2012, they were worth three cents), while the newer ones, which are made almost entirely from zinc, are worth much less. The same idea applies to other coins because they are all made from different mixtures of various metals, depending on the year they were minted. Perhaps surprisingly, recently minted American nickels are actually only 25 percent nickel, and the rest is copper. Maybe nickels should be called *coppers* and pennies *zincs*.

So would trying to do this really be worthwhile? If you could get your hands on 1,000,000 *old* pennies, and the copper is worth three cents, you would make two cents per coin, or $20,000 after melting them down. That's before factoring in the costs for shipping, melting, and everything else. And by the way, all those pennies would weigh about three tons.

While there doesn't seem to be any good way to turn lead into gold, I've known more than a few people who've managed to turn gold into lead.

Web Search Keywords

| *alchemists* | *transmutation* | *coinflation.com* | *stanley miller video* | *melting coin trick* | *coin melt video* |

Chapter 23

Gravity Sucks!

"Gravity, the big G … gotten a hold on me"
—*James Brown, godfather of soul and apparently a Newton fan*

Everybody knows that when you fall down, it feels like the earth is trying to suck you into it. That's because it really is. Gravity wants to bring you to your knees.

That's why it isn't a good idea to jump from a balcony using an umbrella as a parachute, like you see in cartoons. Wile E. Coyote tried it on more than one occasion, and always to bad effect. It's a bit like the classic game of rock-paper-scissors, where rock beats scissors. Gravity beats umbrellas. It turns out that even in cartoons, umbrellas don't offer much of a defense against falling rocks either.

> "How can I escape this irresistible grasp?"
> *Pink Floyd, Learning to Fly*

Airplanes have been around for only a hundred years because it turned out to be pretty tricky to figure out how to keep them up there, defying gravity. It's all been worked out, though. Astronauts have even gone all the way to the moon and back, although Apollo 13 was a bit of a dodgy trip. But it sure made for one great movie.

Try to think like Newton by asking yourself how gravity works, and why you are always getting pulled to the ground.

Objects all share a property called *mass,* which pulls them toward each other. The earth is a pretty big and massive place, so it's got a really strong grip on you. Try jumping up. Although you only feel the earth pulling on you, you are actually pulling it a tiny bit toward you as well. But your effect on the earth is like a match between a flea and a professional wrestler. Let me take that back; it's more like a fight between the flea and 47,000 trillion 250-pound wrestlers, if you want to get the proportions correct.

> "It's a good thing we have gravity or else when birds died they'd just stay up there. Hunters would be confused."
> *Steven Wright*

One good question to ask about gravity would be: "What's it like someplace else?" The answer is that gravity works the same way here as it does everywhere else. Its effect depends on the mass of whatever's pulling you toward it. This is what makes up the concept of weight. Sometimes the words *weight* and *mass* are used interchangeably, but weight is the force of attraction you feel to a massive object like the earth. You could think of weight as a side effect of mass.

If you could somehow get yourself to the moon, even though gravity works the same there as it does here, your weight would be different. That's because the moon is smaller than the earth, so it wouldn't pull you down nearly as much. If you weighed one hundred pounds on earth, you'd feel like you weighed only sixteen pounds on the moon. That's why whenever you see film footage of astronauts, they seem to be half floating as they hop around.

But if you were to travel to Jupiter, the largest and heaviest planet in our solar system, you'd weigh about 2.5 times as much as you do here on earth. So a 200-pound adult would feel like he weighed 500 pounds. And that would make it pretty tough to stand up. That might not seem all that dramatic, given that Jupiter is eleven times bigger than the earth. It's about 89,000 miles in diameter, compared to the earth's 7,900 miles. Jupiter is a gas giant. It's made up mainly of hydrogen and helium, just like the sun. Because of its lighter composition, if Jupiter were the same size as the earth, its mass would be only about one quarter as much.

Here's a question you might ask: "Why isn't Jupiter a star too, if it's made up from much of what makes the sun?"

> "The scientific theory I like best is that the rings of Saturn are composed entirely of lost airline luggage."
> *Mark Russell*

Binary (two-star) systems turn out to be pretty commonplace in the galaxy. Jupiter, however, is only about one eleven-thousandth of the mass of the sun. If it had been much, much bigger, it may well have turned into a star. And if that had been the case, it would have interfered with the evolution of life on earth.

To explore the concept of weight a little further, let's consider *neutron stars*, which are collapsed stars that turn out to be pretty interesting. They weigh about the same as the sun, but they are tiny. Typically, they are only about fifteen miles across, compared to the earth's 7,900 miles or the sun's 860,000 miles. On earth, one teaspoon of its stuff would weigh six billion tons. Six billion tons is hard to imagine. To give you some idea of it, imagine building a railway track using standard rails. (They come in different sizes.) Your railway would need to extend about 26 million miles to weigh that much. That's about one third the distance from the earth to the sun. The gravities of neutron stars are so strong that you would weigh at least 200 billion times what you weigh on earth!

If you were able to drop something from one meter above the surface of a neutron star, it would take one millionth of a second to reach the surface, and it would impact at around 4.5 million miles per hour.

Let's take it over the top.

Stranger still are objects known as black holes. These collapsed stars have been compressed so dramatically that they are just points in space, called *singularities*. Their gravities are so intense that not even light can escape. That's the *black* part. Nothing that gets too close can escape their pull—it just gets sucked in. That's the *hole* part. Your weight there would be infinite; and I don't think there's any diet for that. It has been jokingly said: "Black holes are where God is dividing by zero."

One of the reasons that the earth is such a hospitable planet is its moderate gravity. It holds all the air in close to its surface, but without crushing us at the same time. This is definitely good news for all the plants, animals, and people who live here. On the moon, there's not enough gravity to hold in an atmosphere.

You have to break free of the earth's gravity to get to the moon. The only way to do that is by taking off fast, or by peddling hard along the way, like a rocket. You'd need to take off at about seven miles per second to get away. This is known as *escape velocity.* It means that if you wanted to throw a tennis ball all the way to the moon, you'd have to launch it at around 25,000 mph. That's about 200 times faster than a hard serve from a professional tennis player. The fastest serve on record was in the 2011 Davis Cup, when Ivo Karlovic knocked it at 156 mph. Even so, he'd need to serve it 160 times harder still to hit the moon.

Try to picture it another way.

You should learn to think like Wile E. Coyote once in a while, because it's just plain fun. Let's say you build a long highway with a giant ski jump at the end. A fast sports car can accelerate from zero to sixty in about four seconds. At that rate of acceleration, it would take about half an hour to hit the 25,000 mph that you'd need to break free of the earth's gravity. To do this, you'd need to build a highway that stretched from New York to Tokyo, and you'd need to do some customizing to your car as well. And I'm not just talking about a new paint job.

> "Think off center."
> *George Carlin*

Evel Knievel, eat your heart out. In case you don't know about him, Evel was an American daredevil who attempted enormous ramp-to-ramp motorcycle jumps between 1965 and 1980. In 1974 he even attempted to jump across the Snake River Canyon in a steam-powered rocket; maybe Wile E. inspired him. If you've ever dreamed about getting into the Guinness Book, this is one to miss. He holds the record for most bones broken in a lifetime—433! To put that into perspective, the human body contains only 206 bones.

To break away from a neutron star, you'd have to launch from its surface at around 200 million miles per hour, which is close to one-third of the speed of light.

> "There are doors that let you in and out, ... but they are trapdoors, That you can't come back from"
> *Radiohead*

Escaping from a black hole is a bit trickier. Even though they are believed to be just points, there is something called an *event horizon*, from which, if crossed, there can be no escape. The escape velocity at the event horizon is exactly the speed of light, so even if you could travel at 99.999 percent of light speed, you would still never get away.

Web Search Keywords

| *james brown gravity* | *apollo 13* | *houston we have a problem* | *astronauts bunny hop on the moon* | *rockets* | *saturn V* | *space shuttle launches* | *black holes* | *neutron stars* | *andy kaufman wrestling* | *fastest tennis serves video* |

Chapter 24

What Weighs More?

There's an old riddle that's popular with kids: "What weighs more? A pound of bricks or a pound of feathers?" Of course it's a trick question, because a pound is a pound, so they weigh the same.

A more interesting question would be: "What *falls* faster, something that weighs one pound or two?" People first asked that question a long time ago, and kept on asking it for quite a while.

What do you think? There's an experiment you can try for yourself. It's fun and maybe a bit surprising, depending on your answer to the question in the first place. Take a marble and an apple, and push both of them from a table; better yet, push them from someplace higher. If you push them with a ruler or something like that, you can launch them at the same time to make it a fair race.

> "In many cartoons, everything falls slightly faster than an anvil."
> *Author unknown*

Try it again, but this time use an apple and a piece of crumpled paper. The trouble with the paper is that it has lots of *air resistance*, making it impossible to keep up with the apple. Air resistance is a form of *friction*. It works a lot like rubbing your finger on sandpaper. Friction slows things down. Try it again, but this time press the paper into a tight ball, and maybe wrap it up with masking tape, and watch what happens.

The Ancient Greeks, led by Aristotle, believed that heavier things must fall faster, but for all their wisdom they couldn't possibly have tried it out, because it's easy to spot the answer. The first person to actually try it was Galileo, by dropping objects from the leaning Tower of Pisa. His theory was that objects should all fall at the same speed, regardless of weight, in the absence of air resistance. Because he tested his theory with an experiment, many consider him to be the original physicist. The best experiment to test what falls faster took place on the moon, where there's no atmosphere. Apollo 15 astronaut Dave Scott dropped a hammer and a falcon feather (the lunar module was named the *Falcon*), and they arrived at the same time.

> "I greatly doubt that Aristotle ever tested by experiment."
> *Galileo*

Just for fun, you might try dropping baseballs and watermelons from your upstairs bedroom window. It works the same way, and the watermelons are funny to watch. Just don't tell anyone where you got the idea. Instead, you might look up the David Letterman reference below.

Web Search Keywords

| *david letterman throwing stuff off a roof* | *dropping watermelons* | *monty python dropping things from high places* | *monty python science* | *what falls faster* | *leaning tower of pisa* | *apollo 15 feather hammer* |

Chapter 25

Bankers and Their Adventures with Scientists

"The most powerful force in the universe is compound interest."
—*Albert Einstein, possibly at the suggestion of his banker*

It was always a good idea to pay attention to just about anything Einstein said. While there is some debate over whether he ever actually said that, or if it's just some kind of scientists' urban legend, it's an idea that's certainly worth looking into. Nevertheless, I do know that he must have had at least some interest in money, because he once said, "The hardest thing in the world to understand is income tax."

The idea of compound interest is earning interest on interest, and it has been around for a very long time. You earn interest on savings in a bank account. Bank accounts are a bit like renting out your money. The amount a bank is willing pay to use your money determines the interest rate. The bank in turn lends it out to someone else at a higher interest rate, or maybe invests it in something to earn a profit.

"An investment in knowledge pays the best interest."
Benjamin Franklin

In an episode of *Seinfeld* ("The Junior Mint"), George says, "Yeah interest, it's an amazing thing. You make money without working." Jerry replies, "Y'know I have friends who try to base their whole life on that principle."

Let's make up a number for interest rates; call them 10 percent. They're actually quite a bit lower than that right now, which makes the story less compelling, but using 10 percent will make it easier to get the point across. Here's how your account would grow over time with compounding:

Date	Starting Balance	Interest	Closing Balance
Today	$100	$10	$110
Next year	$110	$11	$121
Next next year	$121	$12.10	$133.10
Another year later	$133.10	$13.31	$146.41
And so on ...			

With compound interest, you keep earning 10 percent on a bigger and bigger balance, so your bank account grows faster and faster. That's because not only do you earn interest on your original deposit, but you also earn interest on all the interest that you earned before. If you start out with $100, after three years you'd have $133 in your account.

Without compounding, or with simple interest, you'd only have $130 ($10 per year over the first three years). While that three-dollar difference might not strike you as a big deal, just wait.

Where compound interest gets interesting, and maybe what caught Albert's eye, is just how fast it can accumulate once it gets going. After ten years, your $100 would have grown to $259, more than twice what you started with. It would be only $200 without

> "When I turned two I was really anxious because I'd doubled my age in a year. I thought if this keeps up by the time I'm six I'll be 90."
> *Steven Wright*

compounding. After 25 years, you'd have $1,083, which is more than ten times what you started with ($350 without compounding). After fifty years it would be worth $11,739 ($600 with simple interest).

After 100 years, you'd be a millionaire, with $1,378,061 in your bank account. Without compounding, it would be only $1,100. Then again, you'd be more than a hundred years old, so you might not care anyway. But your heirs sure would.

There's a story about how Native Americans from the East Coast of the United States sold Manhattan Island in 1626 to a group of settlers for twenty-four dollars worth of beads and trinkets. Bad deal? Well, if you could have taken that twenty-four dollars and somehow managed to compound it at 8 percent over all those years, it would be worth around $177 trillion today.

I'm not entirely convinced that Albert Einstein cared all that much about banking if and when he remarked on compound interest. Rather, I think his point about the importance of compounding was how it relates to other kinds of growth like populations of bacteria, frogs, or even people. They all grow with compounding, based on some growth rate, and work exactly the same way as compound interest. Sometimes people talk about the idea of *doubling time*, which is how long it takes for a population to double in size. At a 10 percent annual growth rate, it takes slightly more than seven years to double.

You might ask yourself if all this could work backwards. The answer is yes. And it happens in nature all the time, though you might never have noticed it. Many of the elements that make up the world are unstable and don't last forever. They kind of melt away, like an ice cube or a bar of soap in the shower, through a process called *radioactive decay*. That may be a difficult concept to imagine at first because it involves nuclear science. While that might sound unsettling, there's no need to worry because it's not really all that complicated.

> "Ketchup left overnight on dinner plates has a longer half-life than radioactive waste."
> *Wes Smith*

The upside down version of doubling time is something called *half-life*. It means that after a specified period of time, you will have only half as much of the stuff that you started with because half of it sort of melted away. It's unfortunate how money can sometimes work that way too, and often with an extraordinarily short half-life.

Radiocarbon dating, or carbon dating, is one practical application that takes advantage of the idea of half-life. And no, it's not about taking a lump of charcoal to the movies. Carbon dating is one way that scientists can determine the age of ancient artifacts. Carbon is an element that makes up much of our world, including everyday things like barbeque coals, the graphite in pencil lead, diamonds, and even burnt bits on a hamburger.

In nature, most atoms come in different forms called *isotopes*. You can think of them as different car models, like the base model and the turbo. Regular everyday carbon is called carbon-12 (written as ^{12}C). The turbo-charged version, carbon-14 (^{14}C), exists in a small proportion to the rest of the carbon out there. The regular carbon-12 (^{12}C) is stable and lasts forever. Its bigger brother, ^{14}C, is unstable and decays over time. The half-life of ^{14}C is about 5,700 years, which means that after 5,700 years, you'd only have half as much as what you'd started with. When ^{14}C decays, it turns into nitrogen and spits out an electron an some energy.

Most of the earth's atmosphere (78 percent) is nitrogen. Most of the rest is oxygen (21 percent), which people and animals need to live. Plants and trees all breathe air, but what they like best is carbon dioxide. Carbon dioxide consists of one carbon atom and two oxygen atoms (that's the *di* in dioxide), and combined, they make up one carbon dioxide molecule. Even though it makes up only about 0.03 percent of the atmosphere, plants and trees end up loaded with carbon.

> "I went out on a radio carbon date. She turned out to be pretty old."
> *Author Unknown*

For a bunch of reasons we don't need to get into here, the mix of ^{12}C and ^{14}C in the atmosphere stays in a roughly constant proportion, and the trees are constantly breathing it. After a tree dies, the ^{14}C is no longer being replenished, and it starts gradually melting away. Because the amount of ^{14}C in the air is exceedingly small, being about one part in a trillion, carbon dating requires some pretty accurate measurements, but it's pretty easy to pull off these days.

You can estimate the age of an ancient piece of wood (which is typically about 50 percent carbon), simply by measuring the ratio of ^{14}C to ^{12}C in it. For example, if there is half as much ^{14}C compared to how much should be there, and knowing that its half-life is 5,700 years, it would be expected to be roughly 5,700 years old. The technique can date as far back as 50,000 years. Scientists first used it to date an Ancient Egyptian barge that sank around 1850 BC. (There was a historical account of the sinking that confirmed the age determined by the technique.)

Radio carbon dating is a branch of science known as *radiometric dating*. It is based on the radioactive decay of other elements in the earth's crust that have much longer half-lives. With it, the earth's age has been calculated as 4.54 billion years old. That's roughly one-third of the age of the universe.

If you remember the baseball paradox from chapter 9, you might ask yourself: "When something is half melted, it always still has half way to melt again, and so on. So how can it ever completely melt?"

One way to shed light on this paradox is by going back to the gambling games that we looked at earlier. In a game like roulette, where I bet on red or black, the Monte Carlo Casino makes, on average, 2.7 percent per spin. If I start out with ten chips, I would win some and lose some, but on average I would lose one chip every thirty-seven spins. So it should take on average 370 spins for me to run out of my ten chips. Actually, it's really more like 330 spins because it's customary to leave a tip before getting up from the table.

But whether it's with chips or with atoms, when you run out, you're done.

Web Search Keywords

| *compound interest calculator* | *half-life* | *science for kids* | *melting ice cube* | *melting ice cubes at 100 times normal speed video* | *radio carbon dating mr. anderson* |

Chapter 26

Aha! Now I Get It

When you think about a problem long enough, sometimes you can suddenly experience a moment of insight that seemingly comes out of nowhere. It's when you say to yourself: "Now I get it!" People call them *Aha! moments*, and they've been around for a long time.

When I was growing up, I sometimes asked myself how a big ship made from steel could possibly float. Many people probably thought about that a very long time ago; and they likely wondered what it was that makes some things float and others sink. Wood floats, so many people wouldn't think it too much of a stretch that a wooden boat could float too.

> "So if she weighs the same as a duck, then she's made of wood and therefore a witch, so burn her! And if she sinks? Burn her anyways!"
> *The Search for the Holy Grail (paraphrased)*

Archimedes, the Ancient Greek mathematician, physicist, engineer, and astronomer, figured it all out about 2,200 years ago. As the story goes, he made his great discovery when he noticed the water level in a bathtub rise as he climbed in. I think the best part of the story is that Archimedes was so excited when he made his discovery that he leapt from the bathtub and ran naked through the streets shouting, "Eureka!" (I have found it!). That makes for one mad scientist.

The rising water level made him realize that it is the displacement of water that makes things float or sink. An apple naturally pushes away the same volume of water as the size of the apple. The object floats if it weighs less than that amount of water. If it weighs more, it sinks. Even a giant aircraft carrier made of steel will float, as long as it's not filled with too many jet fighters. More specifically, Archimedes's buoyancy principle states that a body in water experiences a force equal to the weight of the water that it displaces. That might explain why markers on waterways are called *buoys*. They all float. Otherwise, they wouldn't be too helpful.

The idea of Eureka! or Aha! moments has been the subject of much study. These revelations emanate mainly from the right side of the brain, the side most often associated with creative arts. The left side of the brain is where linear thinking and deductive reasoning take place. Mathematics appears to involve both sides, but different types of math favor one side or the other. For example, precise calculations tie up more of the left, while estimates or rough calculations use more of the right, as they're more intuitive.

After one Eureka! moment, mathematician Carl Friedrich Gauss said, "I have the result, only I do not yet know how to get to it." Gauss was once described as the greatest mathematician since antiquity. He lived until the late 1800s.

Albert Einstein no doubt had many, but one Aha! came when he realized that objects in free fall don't notice gravity. That observation eventually led to his theory of general relativity. He later described this moment of insight as, "The happiest thought of my life."

At one point or another, just about everybody has said: "Let me sleep on it." That's a wonderful idea, because your mind is still very busy even when you rest, and if you're trying to solve a problem, naps might be a good thing too.

When we're out and about, our minds have lots to deal with. Sleep is like the disk cleanup that computers do. Sleep is a time when your brain organizes and refiles your thoughts. One good example is chemist Kekule von Stradonitz, who discovered in 1865 that the chemical benzene has a ring structure. While his conclusion no doubt followed a great deal of thinking, he eventually came up with the idea in his sleep, when he dreamed of a snake biting its own tail.

One of the easiest ways to experience Aha! moments is to spend time on puzzles and similar problems. Every word you solve in a cryptic crossword gives you one. These word puzzles often require interpreting literal meanings on different levels. What's the answer to the clue, "Not seeing window covering?" It appears at the end of the chapter.

Here's another kind of puzzle that illustrates the same point. It's based on an equation using Roman numerals. Represented with matchsticks, it looks like this:

IV = III – I

Taken literally, it would read *4=3-1,* which is mathematically incorrect. The puzzle is to move only one matchstick and make an equation that is true. Aha! moments often come from thinking outside the box, which you'll find is needed here.

Let's get back to Mr. Eureka because there might be more to his story.

Philosophers and scientists all need to earn a living just like everyone. According to legend, Archimedes was hired to figure out if a certain crown was made from pure gold, or if it was a mix of gold and something else like silver. The hitch was that the crown could not be tampered with in any way, such as by taking a small sample to determine its density. Density is how much something weighs divided by its volume. Calculating density is easy for something shaped like a sugar cube because you can easily determine its volume by measuring the length of the sides, but it's a completely different matter for irregularly shaped objects like the crown. Archimedes's trick might have been to figure out the crown's volume by how much water it displaced. By

> "Science is a wonderful thing if one does not have to earn one's living at it."
> *Albert Einstein*

weighing the crown, he then could have easily calculated the crown's density and whether or not it was the same as pure gold.

Or so the story goes. Nobody will ever know. But it makes for an interesting story, and if it's true, makes for one pretty darned good piece of thinking.

Often, you can take a reality check on stories or ideas like that one just by asking relatively simple questions. The question I asked myself was whether the different densities of a pure-gold crown and one mixed with some silver could be possible to measure *in practice*, especially since it took place more than 2,000 years ago.

Here's one way to look at it. As an example, let's take the Imperial State Crown, worn by Queen Elizabeth on her coronation in 1953. It's a pretty fancy one, with lots of diamonds and gems, which we'll have to ignore and pretend it's all gold. It weighs 0.91 kg, which is about two pounds. The density of gold is about twice that of silver. If the Archimedes crown was 25 percent silver, he would have needed to detect only about a 100-gram discrepancy, which is roughly the weight of twenty nickels. That doesn't seem impossible, even though it was thousands of years ago. The point is that if the discrepancy was much smaller, you might have questioned whether the story made any sense at all.

One fun way to illustrate buoyancy at home is to fill up a sink or, better yet, a bathtub. Then fill a Ziploc bag completely with water. Seal it underwater so there's no air trapped inside. It will have a neutral buoyancy so that it can move up or down or just swirl around with all the rest of the water. Next, pull the bag above the surface and let a little air in. After it's resealed, you can see how easy it is to make your makeshift oil tanker float—or I guess *water* tanker in this case.

Have you ever wondered how submarines work? They are able to easily move up and down. Try to figure it out, knowing that they have something called "ballast tanks" equipped with pumps. It's not unlike how fish work. They come equipped with an air bladder that they can fill with some of the oxygen they take out of the water when they breathe. By controlling how much air is in there, fish are able to move up and down or hover.

Another good question you might ask about buoyancy is this: "How fast do things *sink* in water?" It goes back to how Galileo threw objects from the leaning Tower of Pisa. You could try it with a hockey puck and a golf ball next time you're in a swimming pool. Then try other objects, but try to figure it out for yourself ahead of time. Think about that crumpled up paper in chapter 24.

"There is nothing—absolutely nothing—half so much
worth doing as simply messing around in boats."
—*Kenneth Graham, The Wind in the Willows*

Answer 1: Blind. The word means "not seeing," and is also a kind of window covering.
Answer 2: If you move one of the matchsticks from the equals sign to above the minus sign you get this:
! \ / - !!! = ! (4-3=1)

Web Search Keywords
| *monty python shes a witch* | *archimedes eureka* | *buoyancy experiments* | *americas cup boat breaks and sinks video* | *queen elizabeth coronation video* | *aha moments mutual of omaha commercials* |

Chapter 27

Experiments You Can Do in Your Head

There are plenty of experiments that you can do in your head. That turns out to be pretty handy because they save you from firing up Bunsen burners, weigh scales, building billion-dollar particle accelerators, or anything like that.

> "My mind is my laboratory."
> *Albert Einstein*

A lot of people might think that Albert Einstein first thought up "thought experiments"—lots of puns in there, but none intended. He is often incorrectly credited for naming them *Gedankenexperimenten*, but the name had already been around for a while.

He did, however, devise both the special and general theories of relativity using thought experiments. Both were remarkable feats. Much of his genius lay simply in thinking while riding trains on his way to and from work in a patent office in Bern, Switzerland.

He asked himself relatively simple questions. And after years of thought, he came up with amazing answers.

Einstein figured that he spent more than seven years thinking about special relativity. He thought visually and liked to imagine things in physical terms. Einstein said: "If I can't picture it, I can't understand it." I'm sure he must have had some Eureka! moments like Archimedes along the way, but he claimed to have just plodded along and filled in the math later. Apparently, special relativity took him only about five or six weeks to write out, but that was after his seven years of thought. He did, however, reveal that general relativity actually began with a flash of insight. He then spent another seven years figuring that one out too.

His thinking often focused on the results of experiments that he read about. At the time, there was a tremendous flood of experimentation going on. Compared to others, he seemed to have the knack of picking the ones that would lead his thinking in the right direction. He spent much of his time trying to *picture* what was actually going on.

> "I think and think for months and years. Ninety-nine times the conclusion is false. The one hundredth time I am right."
> *Albert Einstein*

Later in life, he became absorbed in trying to create a theory that unified all the forces of nature. Physicists are still trying to solve that one. He moved more and more to thinking mathematically and eventually tried to express his ideas entirely in mathematical terms. This was quite a departure from his old approach of thinking visually and worrying about the math later. Some historians have argued that his change in thinking may have impeded his progress in developing new theories that he worked on throughout the remainder of his life. But hey, those critics were no Einsteins.

Einstein's method of thinking, just asking questions and imagining, had actually been going on for a long, long time. It goes all the way back to the Ancient Greek philosophers and probably even earlier.

Many suggest that Galileo performed a simple thought experiment to conclude that all objects fall at the same rate. His thinking would have been based on a simple question: "What will happen if I take a heavy object like an anchor, tie it to a smaller lighter anchor, and throw the whole package out of the window?"

To answer the question, his reasoning would have strung together a series of other questions:

- If the heavier anchor naturally falls faster than the lighter one, wouldn't the heavier anchor pull the lighter one along with it and speed it up?
- But then wouldn't the lighter anchor slow down the heavier one?
- Then again, isn't the whole combined package just one bigger and heavier thing?
- And if heavier things fall faster, shouldn't that make the whole package fall even faster still?

Because of the apparent contradictions in this chain of reasoning, he correctly concluded that everything must fall at the same rate—all without lifting a finger, just by asking simple questions.

You can make all kinds of discoveries—often simple, though sometimes profound—just by asking questions and picturing the answer. And it's been working for thousands of years.

Web Search Keywords
| *thought experiment examples* | *top 10 thought experiments* |

Chapter 28

Einstein's Relatively Good Questions

"You can choose your friends, but you can't
choose your relatives. That's my relativity."
—Bruce Einstein, A.'s little-known older brother

In 1905, Albert Einstein changed absolutely everything. His ideas created an explosion in physics. It was a nuclear explosion, in fact. You might think of him as Isaac Newton on steroids, although humble Albert would not have agreed. The greatest thinkers are often truly among the most unpretentious of people.

"'Thank you,' the old man said. He was too simple
to wonder when he had attained humility. But he
knew he had attained it and he knew it was not
disgraceful and it carried no loss of true pride."
—Ernest Hemmingway, The Old Man and the Sea

Newton said: "If I have seen further, it is only by standing on the shoulders of giants." I bet Genghis Khan never said anything like that.

It is by publishing papers that scientists relate their ideas and discoveries to each other and the world. In 1905, Einstein became a giant who climbed up on the shoulders of giants by publishing not one, but *four* illustrious papers. At the time, Einstein was about the same age as Newton in his prime, having just turned twenty-six.

> "Sometimes I feel I've got Newton's quote upside down and that 'If I've not seen as far as others, it is because giants are standing on my shoulders.'"
> *Author Unknown*

One day I was thinking about his remarkable achievements in 1905 and asked myself what else was going on back then. I thought it would be useful to put 1905 into some kind of context.

- The Russian Revolution began with Bloody Sunday (1905).
- The then New York Giants beat the Philadelphia Athletics in the World Series (1905).
- Marconi sent and received wireless transmissions between England and Canada, giving rise to the modern radio (1901).
- Queen Victoria died after a reign of sixty-four years (1901).
- The first tyrannosaurus rex fossils were discovered (1902).
- Henry Ford started the Ford Motor Company (1903).
- The New York subway opened (1904).
- Roald Amundsen became the first person to pass successfully through the Northwest Passage (1906).
- Finland became the first country to give women the right to vote (1906).
- Pablo Picasso painted the sublime *Demoiselles d'Avignon* (1907).

It must have been a fascinating period of time to be alive.

Some of the ideas that follow involve a fair bit of math, but there's absolutely nothing wrong with getting the idea and saving the math for later, just like Einstein used to do. So let's climb to 30,000 feet to see what was going on in Einstein's astonishing year.

1. The Photoelectric Effect

On a Heuristic Viewpoint Concerning the Production and Transformation of Light
Submitted: March 8; Published: June 9

Einstein explained something called the *photoelectric effect*, which is how electric currents can be created simply by shining light on certain materials, including metals. Although it was first observed as early as 1839, it was a complete mystery until Albert came along. Solar cells work because of the photoelectric effect.

Standing on the shoulders of giants, especially Max Plank in this case, Einstein explained how light can share the properties of both particles and waves at the same time. It was an important step in the development of quantum mechanics, which we'll get to in the next chapter. He described light as traveling in little packets called *quanta*, which eventually became known as *photons*. When photons strike a material, they can knock electrons free and cause an electric current.

> "Sweet photons, I don't know if you're waves or particles, but you go down smooth."
> *Futurama*

This was the paper that won Einstein the Nobel Prize in Physics in 1921. Some might be surprised at that. But his other theories, including relativity, were still being debated at the time. All were eventually proven to be correct.

The photoelectric effect is used in many applications besides solar cells, including night vision goggles. It's seen in spacecraft and even on the surface of the moon. Sunlight charges dust on the surface, causing it to levitate in a thin suspended layer. A probe first spotted this effect in the late 1960s.

2. Brownian Motion

On the Motion of Small Particles Suspended in a Stationary Liquid, as Required by the Kinetic Theory of Heat
Submitted: May 11;Published: July 18

Einstein's theory of *Brownian motion* is probably the least appreciated of his 1905 papers, but it is just as spectacularly important.

Brownian motion describes the way minute particles move around randomly in a fluid or gas. It's named after Robert Brown, who first observed the phenomenon in the early 1800s. It explains the way smoke coming from smokestacks looks, or like steam coming from sewer grates on a cold day. Although air movements themselves can blow dust particles around, molecules are also hitting them from every direction in a random way, which results in a chaotic motion.

Yet again, the idea actually dates back much further, all the way to ancient Rome, in 60 BC. Lucretius described the random motion of dust particles in a sunlit room and attempted to use it as a proof of the existence of atoms.

Many scientists tried to figure out that crazy motion over the ensuing years, but it took Einstein to formulate the equations that describe it. Einstein's mental leap was to figure out the movement of a single particle within a collection of particles. The results enabled him to determine the sizes of atoms and their weight. It was actually the first theory to confirm the existence of atoms, the building blocks of all matter. Before Einstein, the existence of atoms was still a matter for debate, even though they had been first proposed in ancient Greek science.

Important discoveries often arrive with fresh answers to old questions, and this one had been around for a very long time.

3. Special Relativity

On the Electrodynamics of Moving Bodies
Submitted: June 30; Published: September 26

Albert's most famous work is the theory of relativity, although it's more correctly referred to as the *special theory of relativity.* Special relativity has amazing implications and sometimes makes predictions that defy common sense. It turned hundreds of years of thinking on its head.

> "Newton, forgive me."
> *Albert Einstein*

Special relativity began with Einstein's questions about the nature of light. He asked himself: "What would it be like to ride on a beam of light?"

Experiments had already shown that the speed of light was exactly the same from every direction. It didn't matter where it was coming from or how fast you were moving relative to it. If you were to measure the speed of light from car headlights coming toward you, and then from the taillights going away from you, both speeds would turn out to be identical. How could this possibly be true? You might think that for a car traveling at 60 mph, the speed of light that you saw as it approached would be some speed plus 60 mph, and when the car receded, it should be the same speed minus 60 mph. You would think it should work like the Doppler effect that you hear when a car or train passes by, when the pitch of its horn and other sounds it's making suddenly drops.

Einstein spent years thinking about this paradox; tenacity was one of his strong suits. One of the most widely used illustrations of his insight is based on a thought experiment. Imagine someone traveling on a train when two lightning bolts hit the front and back ends of the train at exactly the same time. How would different observers perceive it?

> "I was in a job interview and I said to the guy, 'Let me ask you a question. If you were driving your station wagon at the speed of light and turned your headlights on, what would happen?' He said 'I don't know.' I said 'I don't want the job.'"
> *Steven Wright*

If you were standing on the platform when the train went by and both strikes hit the front and the back of the train at exactly the same time, you would say the strikes were simultaneous. But to someone who was on the train, like Einstein, the strike at the front would appear to occur slightly sooner than the one at the rear due to the motion of the train.

This inspired him to think that there are no absolute measurements in the universe. Everything depends on who you are, where you're looking from, and how you're moving. It prompted him to think that our clocks must also be different too, which would mean that there is no absolute time. Wow!

We don't usually notice any effects of relativity in our day-to-day lives, but if you were to travel very, very fast relative to me, and if I could somehow manage to see your wristwatch, it would be ticking slower than mine. It's not that it just appears to be that way, it's because time itself is actually passing more slowly for you than it is for me. From that, Einstein also determined that a rod traveling near the speed of light would be shorter from my perspective.

One simple question gave rise to an interesting paradox early on. It became known as the *twin paradox:* "What would happen if there were twins, and while one stayed on earth, the other sped off in a rocket near the speed of light for a couple of years and then returned home?" The paradox was: "Shouldn't both clocks appear to be moving slowly relative to each other?"

It was eventually resolved by the fact that the twin in the spaceship had to turn around to get back to earth. The astronaut twin was the one doing the moving relative to the twin at home. If the ship cruised at a comfortable 85 percent of the speed of light, and the round trip lasted five years, the twin on earth would actually have aged ten years versus five for the traveler. Going faster still, the effect is magnified; when the travelling twin returns, he might well meet his long deceased twin's great-grandchildren.

Just as oddly, moving causes you to weigh more. The faster you travel, the heavier you become. So if you're on a diet, don't travel anywhere near the speed of light, I guess. If you travel at the speed of light, you become infinitely heavy, which is one of many illustrations and explanations that have been used to explain why nothing can travel faster than the speed of light.

While many experiments from the early 1900s had already proven the puzzling effects predicted by relativity, a pair of scientists carried out a simple experiment in 1971 to illustrate *time dilation*, or the slowing down of time arising from relative motion, but in an everyday setting. They placed highly accurate atomic clocks aboard two Boeing 747 jet airliners and flew them around the world in opposite directions. While they weren't traveling anywhere even remotely close to the speed of light, Einstein's effects were still there. They detected a tiny difference in time between the two jets of 200 nanoseconds (billionths of a second), right in line with what relativity predicts.

Special relativity stood alone. It contained no references to other papers or other people's ideas. It was completely new.

4. Mass-Energy Equivalence (*E=mc*^{2})

Does the Inertia of a Body Depend Upon Its Energy Content?
Submitted: June 30; Published: September 26

Ah, a question. And what a question it was.

All his thinking and theories culminated in Albert's most famous equation, $E=mc^2$, and it's an absolute standout.

Energy and mass are interchangeable. That's so remarkably simple and yet so powerful. It reflects a fundamental beauty in nature, and moreover, in Einstein's thinking. In his own words, "When the answer is simple, God is speaking."

To get inside the mind of one of the greatest thinkers of all time, take ten seconds to imagine what it must have felt like to be the first person to write $E=mc^2$ at the bottom of a page.

The speed of light is a very large number and is the c in Einstein's formula. (The symbol was taken from the Latin *celeritas* meaning "swiftness.") When you take a huge number like c, which is approximately 186,282 miles per second (or about 670 million mph), and multiply it by itself (c^2), you get an absolutely colossal number. The m stands for mass and the E is for energy. So if you could take even a tiny bit of mass and somehow convert it into energy, you should be able to release an astonishing amount. If you could convert just one gram of mass (or around half the weight of a dime) completely into energy, it would be enough to power 400 million 60-watt light bulbs for one hour.

But there's always a catch. The *somehow* is the tricky bit, but it can be done. This is how the sun and stars work all the time; it's how nuclear reactors work every day. The hydrogen and helium that make up the sun are always reacting and converting a tiny portion of the sun's mass into energy. You might think of it as a sort of burning. While that's not exactly correct, it'll do for now.

Besides nuclear reactions, all kinds of interactions are going on all around us all the time. Tiny particles are always interacting with each other and releasing energy. A breathtaking visual example of this can be seen if you live in the north. The northern lights (aurora borealis) arise when charged particles from the sun interact with atoms in the upper atmosphere. I will always remember one spectacular display many years ago in northern Canada that was seen as far south as Florida, which probably frightened a lot of people. The same effect has even been seen near the poles of other planets such as Jupiter.

Einstein went on to devise the *general theory of relativity* ten years after the special theory. It is all about gravity and was the *new and improved* version of Newton's universal law of gravitation. It has profound implications about how mass bends the fabric of space and time and was used to predict the existence of black holes. To get there, Einstein likely borrowed from thought experiments about whether heavier and lighter things fell at different rates.

Try to top Einstein's 1905 this year. Einstein asked some of the best questions of all time. If you ask enough good questions, and come up with the answers, maybe you'll have your own 1905. There's no time like the present to get started.

Web Search Keywords

| *einstein* | *einstein's brain* | *special relativity* | *general relativity* | *photoelectric effect* | *brownian motion* | *twin paradox video* | *declassified us nuclear test film* | *trinity test video* | *solar panel farms* | *nuclear aircraft carrier video* | *e=mc2 video* | *coin trick that fooled einstein* |

Chapter 29

How Small Is Small?

You've already read about big and fast and far. That leaves us with small. The question about how tiny things work turns out to be a pretty big one. You're about to explore the world of the very small—the *crazy* small. And what a strange little world it turns out to be down there. The good news is that there's nothing really all that complicated going on. It just turns out to be rather odd, which makes it all the more interesting.

Like so many other ideas we've seen, the question about what stuff is made from goes back all the way to the Ancient Greeks. Democritus (400 BC) first suggested the existence of atoms as fundamental building blocks of matter. Some consider him to be the grandfather of modern science. He is believed to have followed in Zeno's footsteps by raising a sublime paradox. He probably asked himself something like: "If I keep cutting an olive in half, I will eventually end up with nothing. How can nothing be something?" He thought that there must be some small indivisible bit of something that can't be cut up any further, like the pit in an olive.

> "It's a small world after all."
> *Walt Disney*

The smallest atomic particles that might come to many people's minds are hydrogen atoms, which are made up of one proton and one electron. You learn about them in school. Hydrogen comes as a gas in nature (H_2, two combined hydrogen atoms) and is what made the *Hindenburg* fly, float, burn, and crash. Hydrogen reacts violently and explosively with oxygen. The whole disaster could easily have been avoided by using helium instead. Helium floats in the air about as well as hydrogen, but as an inert gas (meaning that it doesn't react with anything), it can never burn up. But helium was considered to be a strategic material at the time and was largely unavailable. I sometimes wonder what Archimedes (the Eureka! guy) would have said if he could have seen a party balloon floating up into the sky.

Ernest Rutherford, who came to be regarded as the father of nuclear science, offered the first modern description of atoms in 1907, two years *after* Einstein's famous 1905 papers. He proposed that atoms are like tiny planetary systems made from tiny particles (people liked to picture them as billiard balls), with electrons happily orbiting a nucleus, their own little sun. It seemed like a pretty good way to picture atoms, because it was so easy to imagine. But there was a flaw in the picture. Eventually a devastating question was raised: "Why don't the electrons spiral into the protons?" This picture of the atom couldn't possibly be right, or else we wouldn't be here. It stands out as another great example of how questions really can change the world. Niels Bohr came to the rescue and saved this brilliant theory six years later, in 1913. For his efforts, he received the Nobel Prize in Physics in 1922. He proposed that only *certain* orbits, or states, were possible, and nothing was possible in between. In 1926, when physicist Werner Heisenberg added more mathematics to Bohr's model, the atom seemed finally to have been figured out.

That was until scientists started to notice some very strange things going on. Particles, such as electrons, appear to act like waves sometimes too. It was just as Einstein had shown how light could act like *both* a wave and a particle (as a packet of energy). Light seemed to be somehow different, so it wasn't all that difficult to accept this odd concept. But how could the stuff that makes up the material world be just as strange?

> "The electron is not as simple as it looks."
> *Lawrence Bragg*

Edwin Schrödinger published an abstract mathematical description of nature, known as the *Schrödinger wave equation*, at around the same time that Bohr and Heisenberg described the atom as a collection of particles. It describes the particles as waves. He probably thought, "If particles can act like waves, why not describe them as waves?" It can be difficult to understand because it explains the world as one of probabilities, really waves of probability, and involves a lot of complicated mathematics. And if Barbie had actually said, "Math is tough," she'd have been right this time. Nevertheless, the wave description turned out to work extremely well.

So just what are tiny things like electrons? Are they particles, waves, or a bit of each? There was much debate between the two schools of thought.

Heisenberg later reconciled the two competing views of waves versus particles. As the story goes, he had an Aha! moment while walking through a park late one evening. He realized that you could never know both the exact position of any tiny particle and its exact momentum (which is its velocity times its mass) at the same time because the mere act of looking upsets it. So if you know the velocity of a particle accurately, then you can't know exactly where it is and vice versa. In other words, you are entitled to only a limited amount of information when you get down to the tiniest of scales. That restriction brings an element of uncertainty into the particle picture of the atom. It became known as the *Heisenberg uncertainty principle*. It turned out that the particle theory was just as fuzzy as the wave theory. In a way, it shares the spirit of Einstein's cosmic speed limit: It seems that some things in the universe are just not allowed.

"Heisenberg might have slept here."
Author Unknown

All this gave rise to a completely new science: *quantum mechanics*. It makes some of the most precise predictions of any theory devised by mankind. It also makes some of the most bizarre predictions, but they have been proven to be correct again and again.

As strange as some of the ideas will probably sound, quantum mechanics has become fundamental to how we've ended up with many of the fantastic things that are part of our day-to-day lives. Transistors and semiconductors run because of quantum mechanics; therefore, without understanding quantum mechanics there would be no computers. Lasers depend on quantum mechanical effects. Moreover, quantum mechanics governs every chemical reaction going on around us and inside our bodies all the time, even the reason the Hindenburg's hydrogen gas exploded. The list goes on.

Quantum mechanics describes a strange world where particles spend most of their time as waves of probability, like a smeared-out existence. Any given particle isn't really at any particular point in space, at any particular point in time; it's everywhere.

This is without a doubt one of the most difficult aspects of quantum mechanics to grasp because it's so hard to shake the way we are inclined to picture things mentally in order to understand and rationalize them. The reality is that it's simply impossible to picture a quantum mechanical world in any physical sense. Even the word *particle* gets our minds conjuring up images of tiny billiard balls, which makes it all the more difficult to give up that way of thinking. That's why I prefer the term *things* when it comes to particles like electrons; because most of the time they're not really particles at all. On the other hand, these tiny things can be particles some of the time. It's just that they become particles only while you look at them. The act of looking forces the change from waves into particles. Once you stop looking, the particles go back to being waves.

> "I think I can safely say that nobody understands quantum mechanics."
> *Richard Feynman*

Quantum mechanics is God's version of hide and seek.

There were a lot of skeptics at first. Even Einstein, whose ideas were critical to the development of the science, didn't ever really take to the idea of quantum mechanics and its probability-based interpretation of nature. He liked to say, "God doesn't play dice." But the idea eventually really caught on.

I asked myself how I could even attempt to explain any of this without mathematics, using just a simple illustration, or maybe a thought experiment. This version is easy because it dispenses with any tricky math and is based merely on tossing coins, which has already provided useful illustrations in previous chapters.

Imagine a magic shoebox that is completely empty except for one tiny *thing* such as an electron. If I had used the term *particle* instead of *thing*, it might tempt you to think of the electron as a Super Ball bouncing around the inside of the box. The electron could be anywhere inside the shoebox at any time, but it is somewhere. In quantum mechanics, there is no particle. The electron exists everywhere inside box, at least until we look at it. Oddly, it can even exist outside the box for brief periods as well.

> "God not only plays dice, but sometimes throws them where they cannot be seen."
> *Stephen Hawking*

Suppose that our only method of "measuring" the position of the electron in the box is by tossing four coins (we might as well call them magic as well), and the electron's location is determined by which way the coins land.

Tails count as zero. Heads count as one. If we add up the four coin tosses, the total could be any number from zero to four. If the total describes the electron's position in the box, then there are five places where we might find it: left edge (zero), left of middle (one), middle (two), right of middle (three), and right edge (four). When we toss the four coins, there are sixteen different ways they can come up, with only one out of sixteen (6 percent) to find it at either of the edges. There are six ways of hitting the middle (38 percent) and four ways of landing either side of the middle (25 percent).

It turns out to be a good idea to use the four coins because it illustrates one aspect of quantum mechanics. When we go looking for the electron, we're most likely to find it somewhere near the middle of the box, although it could show up anywhere. If we had used a single die instead, we'd end up with the Super Ball version, where the ball is equally likely to be at an edge as it is in the middle. In our oversimplified quantum

> "Not here not there not anywhere!"
> *Dr. Seuss*

mechanics, the electron doesn't exist as a particle until we toss the coins (our way of peering into the box) and force the electron into existence as a particle. Only then do we know where it is. After we've measured it and are no longer looking at it, the electron goes back to being a wave and spreads out everywhere within the box until we flip the coins again.

Let's use the same box to illustrate one of the greatest paradoxes in modern physics, an absolute killer, both literally and figuratively. It's known as *Schrödinger's cat,* an idea that questions reality in a quantum mechanical world. Ironically, Schrödinger himself devised it to raise a couple of subtle points. It involves the possibility of killing a cat, so I thought it might be better to recast it more humanely, but the idea is more or less the same. I call it the *exploding box.* Einstein once used an unstable powder keg as an example in a letter to Schrödinger, so maybe it's not such a bad idea after all.

Let's say that our magic shoebox still contains the one electron from before. Then we add in a magic electron detector.[1] The detector is attached to explosives and placed at the left end of the box. If the electron shows up at the detector when we look (four tails), the box explodes.

In our quantum mechanical box, the electron exists everywhere inside and has a 6 percent chance of showing up at the left edge. But nothing happens until we flip the coins to observe the electron by forcing it from a wave into a particle. So what's really going on inside the box before we flip the coins? How can the box be a bit exploded and unexploded at the same time? To get your mind around this, you have to accept again the fact that you can never really picture reality at that tiny scale.

What Schrödinger might well have had in mind with his paradox was to caution comparing the world of the small with our everyday world. Things are just different down there. It's pointless to try to apply any of our experience and common sense from up here to the world down there.

1 There's a subtle reason why the electron detector has to be *magic*. Observers that force waves into particles don't have to be actual people. Any kind of measurement will do.

Quantum mechanics changed philosophy. Before it arrived, there was a nagging problem in philosophy regarding the idea of free will. After Newton, it was argued that, at least in principle, if you could know every particle that makes up the universe, including everything that we're made from, and all their positions and velocities, all their subsequent movement could be predicted. If that were the case, the future would be predetermined, and free will would be impossible. Philosophers immediately took to the idea of quantum mechanics because its element of uncertainty solved the problem of *determinism* (the idea that everything is predetermined). When you can reasonably introduce uncertainty into the description of the world, determinism simply falls away. And thank goodness for that, because who would want to live in a world like the film *Groundhog Day*?

Quantum mechanics might seem strange at first, but when you think about it, it can begin to make sense. You just have to change your thinking.

> "I used to be a quantum mechanic, but I could never find the car. Albert eventually talked me out of that line of work. So I moved to Vegas and became a dealer. You need to understand probability there as well."
> —*Bruce Einstein, A.'s little known older brother*

Web Search Keywords

| *quantum mechanics video* | *quantum mechanical effects* | *hindenburg* | *microscope pictures* | *hydrogen* | *talking breathing helium* | *electron microscope video* | *schrodinger's cat video* |

Chapter 30

Does the Flap of a Butterfly's Wings in Brazil Set Off a Tornado in Texas?

That odd question marked the beginning of an entirely new science called *chaos theory*. It was the title of a 1979 presentation to the American Association for the Advancement of Science by Edward Lorenz. He was a mathematician, meteorologist, and in the early 1960s, a pioneer in trying to predict weather with computer models. His work led him to question the feasibility of ever making long-range weather predictions. These days, many believe that forecasts longer than one week are meaningless.

> "Chaos is a friend of mine."
> *Bob Dylan*

Chaotic motion had been noticed for many years, even as far back as 500 BC. Einstein described Brownian motion, the crazy motion you see in dust particles in a sunlit room. Later, quantum mechanics threw uncertainty into the mix, with its probability-based description of nature. Although in 1678, Newton's laws had introduced order and structure to explain how the universe works—like an enormous clock with simple underlying mechanisms—there seemed to be more going on. One nagging problem in physics hinted at an early form of chaos theory. Henri Poincaré studied the *three-*

body problem in the late 1880s. It was an attempt to describe the orbits of three bodies like the earth, the moon, and the sun. Anyone can clearly see that there doesn't appear to be any *problem* when it comes to those three bodies, but Poincaré found that in some configurations, the orbits of three bodies could be irregular and impossible to determine.

The term *chaos* is usually taken simply to mean disorder and randomness, but in *chaos theory* it means much more than just a mess. Lorenz had discovered that in unstable systems like the weather, even the most minute disruptions today can lead to *dramatic* differences in what might result later on.

As happened with many important discoveries and inventions, Lorenz came across chaos theory entirely by accident. How ironic! The story is that he decided to rerun one of his computer weather simulations. To save time—computers were pretty slow back then—he restarted the program in the middle of the run by reentering data from the halfway point in the previous run. Because he typed in 0.506 instead of 0.506127, the data wasn't *exactly* the same as before, even if off by only a tiny fraction. To his surprise, he found that the resulting forecast was dramatically different from what he had obtained earlier. It seemed that even a meaningless upset could change everything.

A simple illustration of chaos that you can try for yourself appears at the end of the chapter and its results are quite striking.

Chaos theory got its start by explaining how easily disorder can arise in even the simplest systems that would be expected to be stable. If chaos is inevitable, why is the world the way it is? And how can there be any order at all? Lorenz later found that there *is* order imbedded within the disorder of some seemingly chaotic systems—predictable disorder. It turns out that order and chaos are just two sides of the same coin. Simple rules can lead to order, chaos, or sometimes a mix of the two.

> "Chaos is the score upon which reality is written."
> *Henry Miller*

Around the same time that Lorenz made his discovery, an entirely new geometry arrived on the scene. Fractal geometry is based on *self-similar* structures. These are structures that look the same when viewed on different scales. One good analogy is the way that *Russian dolls* work. Inside each doll is another identical, but smaller, doll.

Benoît Mandelbrot, who is regarded as the father of fractals, kicked off this new science in a 1967 paper in *Science* with a title that began with the question: "How long is the coast of Britain?" The answer turns out to be trickier than you might think, because it depends on the length of the measuring stick used to carry out the measurement. Coastlines are highly self-similar—a magnified view of a very small portion of the coastline looks strikingly similar to the larger view of the entire coast. The deeper you look, the more intricate the coastline becomes. On a coast there are bays, and bays within those bays, and so on. Mathematically, the length of fractal shapes measured at smaller and smaller scales becomes larger and larger, so the idea of length doesn't apply in any conventional sense when it comes to self-similar structures and the world of fractals.

The idea of self-similar structures came up long before fractals. Helge von Koch, a Swedish mathematician, described an interesting shape in 1904 that became known as the *Koch snowflake.* It starts with an equilateral triangle, then adds on smaller one-third-size triangles to each of the three sides, and then smaller ones to the twelve resulting new sides, and so on, to eventually produce a shape that resembles a snowflake. Like the British coastline, its perimeter becomes immeasurable at increasingly small scales. There are many vivid examples of these kinds of shapes available on the Web. They illustrate how formulas can give rise to patterns and pictures.

Mandelbrot's seemingly simple question about coastlines had far-reaching implications because, when you think about it, nothing in nature is smooth. Besides coastlines, fractals are everywhere in nature. They give rise to the forms and patterns you see in trees, snowflakes, branching of streams into rivers, mountain ranges, waves on the ocean, and human blood vessels, to name just a few. Mandelbrot wrote in his book *The Fractal Geometry of Nature*: "Clouds are not spheres, mountains are not cones, coastlines are not circles, and bark is not smooth, nor does lightning travel in a straight line." What child hasn't noticed that when you stick a small branch into the ground it looks just like a miniature tree?

Mandelbrot introduced the mathematical idea of *fractional dimension* to explain and describe the complexity of a self-similar structure. Fractional dimension became the way to describe the *roughness* in nature and gave us a new way of looking at the world. *Fractional dimensions* eventually gave rise to the name *fractal*, which Mandelbrot coined in 1975. The idea that an object can have a fractional dimension isn't as crazy as it first might sound. Everyone knows that a line or curve is one-dimensional and that a plane has two dimensions. So it might not be completely surprising that complex shapes like coastlines fit somewhere in between. Mandelbrot calculated that the west coast of Great Britain has a fractional dimension of 1.25, or roughly the same as a Koch snowflake at 1.26.

How can geometry fit into chaos theory? It turns out that fractals are often the remnants of chaos and can help identify order in chaos. Finding order in complex systems provides more information than statistical methods and can help to make better predictions about possible future behavior.

Fractals have now been applied to a wide range of fields including: physics, engineering, economics and financial markets, biology, population dynamics, philosophy, and meteorology. Cell phones, for example, operate with antenna designs based on fractals. Fractals have profound implications for evolution and one day might explain how DNA *really* works. One very familiar application of fractals is in animation and special effects to generate realistic-looking terrains for applications like video games. Behind all this is just simple math and self-similarity.

You read in chapter 4 how our minds seem to be hardwired to seek out order in chaos. One example came from the mesmerizing appeal—at least mesmerizing to some—of some modern art, such as the works of Jackson Pollock, "Jack the Dripper." Critics often dismissed his work as nothing more than a crazy mess and sometimes even described it as, "Something a trained chimpanzee could do." Researchers, however, have shown that Pollock's work contains

> "Art, in itself, is an attempt to bring order out of chaos."
> *Stephen Sondheim*

fractals because the drips, swirls, and patterns are repeated on different scales. One good example is a painting entitled *Number 14.* It has a high degree of self-similarity and is even more mathematically complex than the west coast of Britain, with a fractal dimension of 1.45. Where did all his different scales come from? Some think that it resulted from the way he painted. He incorporated swirls, splashes, sprays, and poured paint as he moved around the canvas that lay on the floor. If he appeared to paint in a chaotic way, order came out of the chaos not by chance, but through his unknowing use of fractals. To many, Pollock's *drips* are as aesthetically pleasing as anything we see in nature.

Perhaps fittingly, the idea of fractal geometry may have come from art. Mandelbrot's ideas were partly inspired by *The Face of War*, a painting by surrealist Salvador Dali. It depicts a miserable, disembodied face floating above a barren desert. Inside its eye sockets and anguished mouth are more images of the same picture, and so on, just like nested Russian dolls.

While still in its infancy, some maintain that chaos theory might one day be viewed as one of the most important ideas to come out of the twentieth century, alongside relativity and quantum mechanics.

Einstein said, "When the answer is simple, God is speaking," It seems to work the other way around in chaos theory: "When simple rules produce complicated results, God is shouting."

How to make chaos on a computer, if you're so inclined

It's easy to illustrate the idea of chaos with nothing more than simple arithmetic. It uses *mappings* that describe how to produce a sequence of numbers. One very simple example of mapping would be written as $x \leftrightarrow x+1$, where the "$\leftrightarrow$" reads as "maps to" and is a form of an algorithm. This particular mapping means that when you start with any given number, the mapping generates that number plus one. So, when you iterate the process, or keep repeating it over and over again, 1 maps to 2, and then 2 maps to 3, and so on, resulting in: 1, 2, 3, 4 …

The simplest and most frequently illustrated example of a chaotic system that comes from the study of populations is described by the mapping $x \leftrightarrow 4x(1\text{-}x)$. If you were to start with 0.2, it would generate 0.64 (being 4(0.2)(1-0.2)), and the next one would be 0.92, followed by 0.29, 0.82, and so on. With this mapping, and starting with 0.2 as above, you end up with a sequence of numbers that fluctuate between zero and one, in a very "wiggly" and unstable pattern. You have just created chaos with simple arithmetic. What makes it chaotic is that it's extremely sensitive to the initial starting value. If you change the 0.2 by even just one ten-millionth to 0.2000001, it has profound effects on how the pattern unfolds. The two values move in lockstep for a while, but after about twenty steps, small differences start to appear, and then everything breaks down, and the values diverge widely. And remember, this results from the simplest of arithmetic, without any tricky formulas or random chance.

It's simple to do this on a spreadsheet, if you're inclined to see it for yourself. You'll discover that if you change the variables too much, the chaos can go away, and you're left with stable systems where the two predictions agree perfectly.

Web Search Keywords

| *jackson pollock fractals* | *the face of war* | *koch snowflake* | *fractal art video* | *deepest mandelbrot zoom* | *fractals in nature video* | *fractals fern* | *double pendulum video* | *3D terrain generation video* | *pollock painting video* | *salvador dali what's my line* |

Chapter 31

What to Ask about Yourself

ΓΝΩΘΙ ΣΑΥΤΟΝ (Know Thyself)
—*Ancient Greek aphorism*

You might remember a line from chapter 1: "The word *why* is one of the most important and powerful words in the English language—except for *me*. Just kidding, of course."

"Except for *me*" was intended for fun, but maybe it's not all that far off the mark. While you should always ask questions about what's going on in the world around you, you should also ask about the world within you.

"Know thyself" first appeared inscribed on the walls near the entrance to the Temple of Apollo at Delphi.

> "Take one big look, take a look at yourself.... You dig?"
> *Guru, Jazzmatazz*

There were actually three maxims inscribed there. The other two were: "Nothing too much," and "Give surety, get ruin." The latter begs some explanation. It meant that if you borrow money and can't repay it, you become a slave. I'm not sure that things have really changed all that much over the ensuing thousands of years. In Shakespeare's play *The Merchant of Venice*,

Shylock the moneylender demands repayment of his loan by way of a pound of Antonio's flesh, which was part of their deal.

Nobody knows where "Know thyself" really came from, but it has been attributed to many philosophers, most notably Socrates and Pythagoras. Its meaning is still debated even now because sometimes things get lost in translation. On the surface it's about self-awareness, but given its place on the entrance to a temple, some have argued that it's intended as an admonition to be temperate. Others believe it implies that you shouldn't boast about being more than what you are. Some also say it means to pay no attention to popular opinion. In other words, always question things. In that case, the inscription could have better read: "Know for thyself."

> "There are three things extremely hard: steel, a diamond, and to know one's self."
> *Benjamin Franklin*

Philosopher Thomas Hobbs coined the term "Read thyself" in *The Leviathan,* which dates back to 1651. In it he suggested that you could learn about yourself by asking about the feelings that motivate your thoughts and actions.

Always go back to the Five Qs. Thoughtful people ask themselves questions like, "*Who* am I, and *what* do I want to become?" "*Why* do I want it?" and *"How* am I going to get there?"

One of the best questions to ask about you is "How will my obituary read?"

An incredibly compelling story that illustrates self-examination is based on the life of Alfred Nobel, who lived in the late 1800s and is the man behind the Nobel Prize. Alfred was a Swedish chemist and engineer who owned a chemical company and later became an armaments manufacturer. He held 355 patents, but dynamite was his big one. He became wealthy by asking a simple question.

> "If you don't know where you're going, you'll end up someplace else."
> *Yogi Berra*

First you need to know that his chemical company manufactured nitroglycerin, which is unstable and highly explosive. It's pretty nasty because it can explode if you shake it up even just a little. That's not unlike some people I know.

Bottles containing nitroglycerin were always packed in crates filled with sawdust to reduce the impact of any upsets during shipping. It was noticed that sometimes bottles had been broken during delivery and the nitroglycerin had soaked into the sawdust. Surprisingly, they didn't explode. The question of why they didn't blow up is what probably gave rise to Nobel's invention of dynamite, which is a stabilized version of nitroglycerin.

The most intriguing part of his story came about when one of his brothers died while on a visit to Cannes in the south of France. The French media confused his brother with Alfred and made a pretty big deal out of his alleged death with headlines like "The merchant of death is dead" and went on to say, "He became rich by finding ways to kill more people faster than anyone ever before."

Upon reading his premature obituary, Alfred reflected on his life. He went on to leave his massive wealth to establish the prizes that recognize achievements in physics, chemistry, medicine, literature, and what became the peace prize. The prize in economics was added later.

> "The rumors of my death are greatly exaggerated."
> *Mark Twain*

Alfred created the peace prize from the inspiration of a former lover. Even though she had jilted him for another man, she continued to keep in touch with him for the rest of his life.

"I'd kill for a Nobel Peace Prize."
—*Steven Wright, Comedian*

Web Search Keywords
| *merchant of venice youtube* | *alfred nobel youtube* | *nitroglycerin experiments* | *vintage nitro dragster warm up* |

Chapter 32

Ask a Little—Listen a Lot

"I like to listen. I have learned a great deal from listening carefully. Most people never listen."
—Ernest Hemmingway, Nobel Prize in Literature (1954)

You've already seen the importance of asking questions and how much they can help you learn and discover new things. That's only part of the story, because you've got to listen too.

In Asian philosophy, the concept of Yin and Yang embodies how opposite forces can be intertwined, interdependent, and how they can support each other. Asking and listening are a lot like that. When you ask questions of others, or even of yourself, always listen very carefully to the answers.

> "They talk when they should listen."
> *The Godfather*

Asking and listening are different modes of thinking. Imagine your brain as a sponge. When you speak it's like squeezing the sponge out. When you listen, you are supposed to be soaking in. It's essential to focus intently on what the other person is

> "Its very important in life to know when to shut up."
> *Alex Trebek*

saying and not to let your mind drift into thinking about how you're going to respond. Chief Executive Officers (CEOs), the leaders of large corporations, are known to be great questioners, but the best ones are great listeners too. I've heard it said that their listening can sometimes feel like a vacuum cleaner pointed at your head. Here's an important point that many people just don't seem to get. When you're listening, keep your mouth shut. It's as simple as that. You can't soak and squeeze that sponge at the same time. Don't interrupt. Just let people finish what they've started to say. In groups, sometimes it's a good idea just to keep quiet and listen.

None of us communicate as well as we could, so to become a great listener, you've also got to learn to sometimes interpret what people are trying to say. Afterward, you can always ask to make sure you got it right.

All of us are guilty of being poor listeners at least some of the time, especially when we're trying to make a point. I'm no different, so don't listen to me about listening. Instead, I offer the advice of some great listeners:

> "That man's silence is wonderful to listen to."
> *Thomas Hardy*

"We have two ears and one mouth so that we can listen twice as much as we speak."
—Epictetus, *Ancient Greek philosopher and sage*

"It is greed to do all the talking but not to want to listen at all."
—Democritus, *Ancient Greek philosopher*

"If speaking is silver, then listening is gold."
—Turkish proverb

"Listen to many, speak to a few."
—William Shakespeare

"He that speaks much is much mistaken."
—Benjamin Franklin

"Courage is what it takes to stand up and speak; courage is also what it takes to sit down and listen."
—Winston Churchill

"Know or listen to those who know."
—Baltasar Gracian, Spanish Jesuit *and* baroque *prose writer*

"Bore, n. A person who talks when you wish him to listen."
—Ambrose Bierce, *journalist and satirist*

"You aren't learning anything when you're talking."
—Lyndon B. Johnson

"To listen is an effort, and just to hear is no merit. A duck hears also."
—Igor Stravinsky, *composer*

"The most important thing to do is really listen."
—Itzhak Perlman, *violinist and conductor*

"You cannot truly listen to anyone and do anything else at the same time."
—M. Scott Peck, *American psychiatrist*

"Well I have a microphone and you don't, so you will listen to every damn word I have to say!"
Adam Sandler

"There is only one rule for being a good talker—learn to listen."
—Christopher Morley, *journalist, writer and poet*

"Listen to the sound of silence."
—Paul Simon, *singer and songwriter*

Chapter 33

One Last Thought—Think!

"Those who know how to think need no teachers."
—*Mahatma Gandhi*

You've seen that the best way to learn and to discover things comes from asking questions and listening. After all your questioning and listening comes the time to just think and digest it all.

Piglet: I've been thinking …
Pooh: That's a very good habit to get into, Piglet.
—*Winnie the Pooh*

Here's a thought about thinking, and how to make learning, whether it's in high school or college, faster and easier. You might be surprised by how well it can work for you. It works best for sciences involved with numbers and equations as in physics, mathematics, or chemistry, and is based on working backwards.

> "All that we are is the result of what we have thought. The mind is everything. What we think, we become."
> *Buddha*

While some educators might disagree with this approach, it goes like this. The next time you pick up a textbook and have to plow through chapter 5, don't even bother to read it. Nobody wants to read straight through a textbook. It's not a mystery novel, even though it may feel that way sometimes. Instead, just skip straight to the questions at the end of the chapter and try to answer them. In a way, it's not unlike having the book play the role of Socrates. You might not get very far on your first attempt because the questions are probably about new ideas and concepts that you don't happen to know just yet. That's okay, because you can simply go back to the text and figure out how to answer each of the questions one at a time. The questions at the end of any chapter in any decent textbook are about the concepts that the writer thinks are important and what you need to learn. By working through the questions, and once you get all the important ideas under your belt, you can always flip through the text later to pick up the finer points. By then, it'll make for light reading. It takes a bit of work, but if it works for you, it could really pay off.

This approach also works well in other subjects, as long as you apply it the right way. When you study subjects that require opinions, descriptions, and essays, many of the best teachers and professors make use of the Socratic method, which you might remember from chapter 1. It consists of learning by asking and answering questions.

> "I didn't fail the test, I just found 100 ways to do it wrong."
> *Benjamin Franklin*

I came to know a wonderful elderly professor years ago, when I was in college, who might be better described as a *sage*. He gave me a little secret that helped me get through my non-science courses. "In the Socratic method," he said, "learning all comes down to asking and answering questions, right?" I agreed. "So in your lectures, instead of frantically writing down everything the professor has to say, concentrate on the questions that the professor raises in class. Maybe record them on the left hand side of your notebook. These are going to be the ones you're asked on the final exam."

One last thought.

If you ever feel bored, ask yourself questions about anything you see or whatever just pops into your head. Then go and try to figure

> "A mind always employed is always happy."
> *Thomas Jefferson*

out the answer. Sometimes it takes a bit of work, and maybe even quite a bit of research, but that's all pretty easy these days thanks to Google and Wikipedia. And you should know that libraries are still great places to visit.

Learn to learn by asking questions, and learn to listen too—it will change your life for the better and will change it forever.

That's the end for me, but I hope it's only the beginning for you.

"A conclusion is the place where you got tired of thinking."
—*Steven Wright, comedian*

Further Reading

"The more you read, the more things you will know.
The more that you learn, the more places you'll go."
—*Dr. Seuss, I Can Read with My Eyes Shut!*

The Book of Questions, Stock, G. (1987)
Chaos: Making a New Science, Gleick, J. (1987)
The Drunkard's Walk: How Randomness Rules Our Lives, Mlodinow, L. (2008)
The Elegant Universe, Greene, B. (1999)
The Feynman Lectures on Physics, Feynman, R. (1964)
Fooled by Randomness: The Hidden Role in Life and in the Markets, Taleb, N. N. (2004)
Mathematics 1001: Absolutely Everything That Matters in Mathematics in 1001 Bite-Sized Explanations, Elwes, R. (2010)
Paradoxes, Sainsbury R. M. (2009)
Principles of Quantum Mechanics, Shankar R. (1994, 1980)
The Selfish Gene, Dawkins, R. (1976)
Struck by Lightning, Rosenthal, J. (2005)
Surely You're Joking Mr. Feynman: Adventures of a Curious Character, Feynman, R. (1985)
Time Travel and other Mathematical Bewilderments, Gardner, M. (1988)
Why Does $E=mc^{2:}$ *And Why Should We Care?*, Cox B. and Forshaw J. (2009)

Index